WHY NOT FORGIVE?

An Action Plan to Peace and Freedom

Cassie J Williams

© Copyright 2023 by Cassie Jones Williams

All rights reserved. This book or any portion thereof may not be reproduced, stored in a retrieval system, or transmitted, in any form or by any means, electronic, mechanical, photocopying, recording, or otherwise, without prior written permission of the author except for the use of brief quotations in a book review or scholarly journal.

Due to the dynamic nature of the Internet, any web addresses or links contained in this book may have changed since publication and may no longer be valid. The views expressed in this work are solely those of the author and do not necessarily reflect the views of the publisher, and the publisher hereby disclaims any responsibility for them.

Publishing Consultant:

SL Elite Publishing

451-D East Central Texas Expy, Suite 276

Harker Heights, TX 76548

ISBN (Paperback): 979-8-9876748-0-2

ISBN (EBook): 979-8-9876748-1-9

Author: Cassie J. Williams

Edited by: Shirley LaTour

Interior Design by: Shirley LaTour

For your editing, formatting (interior design), and/or book cover needs, email support@slelitepublishing.com www.slelitepublishing.com

Photographer: Cora Zach

Scripture quotations marked AMP are taken from The Amplified Bible Old Testament. © 1965,1987 by the Zondervan Corporation. The Amplified Bible, New Testament © 1954,1958, 1987 by the Lockman Foundation. Used by permission. All rights reserved.

Scripture quotations marked ESV are from the ESV® Bible (The Holy Bible, English Standard Version®), copyright © 2001 by Crossway Bibles, a publishing ministry of Good News Publishers. Used by permission. All rights reserved.

Scripture quotations marked NIV are taken from the Holy Bible, New International Version. NIV. Copyright 1973, 1978, 1984, by International Bible Society. Published by Zondervan, Grand Rapids, Michigan 49530. All rights reserved.

Scripture quotations marked NLT are taken from the Holy Bible, New Living Translation, copyright © 1996, 2004, 2007, by Tyndale House Publishers, Inc. Carol Stream, Illinois 60188. All rights reserved. Website.

Scripture quotations marked KJV are taken from the Holy Bible, King James Version. A Regency Bible. Copyright © 1990 by Thomas Nelson, Inc. All rights reserved.

KJV Life in the Spirit Study Bible. Grand Rapids, Michigan: Zondervan. Copyright: Life Publishers International, 1992, 2003.

Contents

Acknowledgments	xi
Foreword	xiii
Introduction	xvii
1. Two Anecdotes	1
2. The Christian Life	13
3. Speak Your Hurt	33
4. Forgiveness And Humility	51
5. Faith and Forgiveness	67
6. Forgiveness' Opened Door	87
7. Finding a Purpose for Forgiveness	95
8. The Forgiveness Influence	111
9. The Fishing Analogy	127
10. The Power of Forgiveness	139
Prayers	153
Helpful Resources	157
Other books by the Author	161
About Cassie Williams	163

Dedication

*With unconditional love and gratitude,
I dedicate this book to my parents: Preston Jones and
Jannie Johnson Jones;
and siblings: Deidre, Preston Jr., and Gina.*

Acknowledgments

It only takes one person's belief in you to turn things around. As I consider everyone who has invested in my life, past and present, I realize there are far too many to thank individually. However, Darell, Faith, Candace, Elijah, and Ru, thank you for your patience and understanding of the heart I have put into this work. You've helped me fuel the fire that inspired me to continue writing.

My "Prayer Warriors"—Laura Hatten, LaTonya Robinson, Mary Mason, Giovanna Feliciano, Vanessa Hall, and Dr. Zoe Grant: With the crossing of our paths, I am blessed to have your prayers that keep watch over my soul. Your encouragement and prayers have undergirded me in the trenches of the battle.

Thank you, "Lady V" Singleton, for being authentic. I will never forget the first time we met. From that day until now, I still stand by my words, "Everybody needs a Verna." Thank you to those who have trusted me with your story. Trust is one of the greatest values in life.

Their names have been disguised within the book for confidentiality.

A special note of gratitude to Christine H. Boldt for your diligence in proofreading and editing my first draft, your encouragement, and service to the community. Shirley LaTour and SL Elite Publishing provided valuable editorial feedback as drafts were transformed into the final version.

Lord, thank you for trusting me with your voice. You have been my very present help in my time of need. I love you with all my heart.

Foreword

In 2016, on a weekday, during lunchtime, I sat down in a dining booth to have lunch with my new friend, Cassie Williams. As I recall, it was Cheddar's restaurant (I can tell you what we ate, but those fine prints pale in comparison to our heart-to-heart discussion about life, relationships, and our Beloved Father God). Over the past six years, I have watched Cassie navigate through storms that have chased her down and storms she chased down.

I could tell you about her consistent hutzpah to declare war on the enemy of our souls when he came after her marriage, her children, her grandchildren, her ministry, and her friendships. And while all these factual experiences are noteworthy, I would be remiss if I didn't highlight the unrelenting drive Cassie has in prayer and spiritual improvement. You will get a sense for her drive in *Why Not Forgive?*. She reeks saliently with determination in supporting the reader on their pathway to being forgiven and to extend forgiveness.

She has the knowledge, skills, and abilities to develop this groundwork for forgiveness, not only in her personal triumphs but in her professional endeavors as chaplain, counselor, pastor, and ordained minister, as well as a devoted wife and passionate mother (the role of wife and mother could satisfy her credibility by itself).

As a Christian counselor, ordained minister, and certified life coach, I face-off with people every day who are trapped in a dungeon of unforgiveness. Theirs are dungeons dug deeply within their hearts and minds because they have waited far too long to confront their offender; and, they are stuck in apathy, stuck in cold heartedness, stuck in pain. And let me tell you that digging their way out of their dungeon is painstakingly arduous coupled with being clueless on just how to forgive when so much time has passed by, and now they need forgiveness for their own self-afflicted offenses.

It is real analogies like the dungeon that grips at the heart of counselors like myself. I have asked clients many times, *Why Not Forgive?* It is obviously clear to me, as a counselor, that unforgiveness is a hard road to tow for people. It is not that the dungeon is inevitable for people who hold grudges or are stuck in past hurts. I have found that breakthrough happens when folks roll up their sleeves and seriously get to work on the labyrinth of forgiveness: for yourself and your offender.

We appreciate you, Cassie Williams, for sharing your personal narrative in *Why Not Forgive?* of how you dug yourself out of your dungeon of unforgiveness. The fact that you have overcome begrudging your dad to now seeing clearly on prioritizing forgiveness – in due time – provides credibility for this informative and provocative guide you are sharing with the world. You have given us space to own our pain to make that same pain work to our advantage, for us and for whomever the good Lord places in our path.

You have asked tough questions that poignantly give us guidance to forgive and be forgiven. That is what people need – guidance – and playing it safe will not provide structure needed for forgiveness. The forgiveness pathway for readers has been laid out – spiritually, relationally, emotionally, and psychologically. As you read, know that guidance has been laid out for you to triumph over the caustic rule of unforgiveness.

Vanessa Hall
Christian Counselor, Certified Life Coach
Founder of JUST US LIMITED
Helping People Achieve a Functional & Healthy Life
www.justuslimited.com

Introduction

Forgiveness is strong medicine. When the right medication is taken correctly, and ingested, the lasting effect is wholeness in health. Anger, hate, and grudges are everyday life affairs to many people. Unfortunately, I have realized these words mean a lot more. I have learned the different phases and stages of forgiveness and anger.

This blueprint, however gruel, shaped me and defined too much—my childhood, teenage life, and a portion of my adult life. Many have been wounded by "friendly fire" along this journey. Intentional or not, the cut runs deep, and the pain is lamentable. I realize that forgiveness requires way more than a mere pardon. It's a process some give up on. Others forgive but hold on to hurt and pain. A few learn the lesson later on in life, but at least they learn it.

This book, *Why Not Forgive,* summarizes my pain, past, lessons, and regrets. I had a pretty rough start and struggled hard with almost everything. I worked on my thoughts, relationship with God, and ability to forgive, among other shortcomings. I thought these incidents were peculiar until I saw and heard different stories. Then, after studying the cases, I discovered that we all had common ground—we all were sickened at how much we were pushed to the limits regarding forgiveness.

Lift the smoke screens, and take off the mask. Let's be honest with ourselves. We are human and need to change what needs to be changed. My regrets were weighty enough to push me into pouring out my heart in this book. Yet, I know I never felt that sense of balance or completion. I also asked myself some tough questions. How much does it take for God to forgive me daily? How much does it take for Him not to give up on me after many attempts to re-route the path opposite His choosing? How could I expect him to forgive my offenses when I failed to pardon others?

My friend, there's so much life has to offer. Regrettably, a grudge might blindfold you to them. It's okay not knowing where to start or where to end. It's okay if you find it hard to forgive. The concepts presented in this book were written as a stratagem, acquainting you with the need-to-know principles and directing you on the paths to take. I fused my life experiences and lessons to clarify and let you know you are not alone. So read carefully with your mind open and free to learn.

You can forgive. Just believe that!

CHAPTER 1
Two Anecdotes

"It doesn't matter what he did or didn't do... he's still your father."

Or so I thought as the sky darkened, and the crickets took that as a cue to start their choruses. My sister Gina and I stood by the road, our hearts thudding with heightened anticipation. Had our father lost track of time? Had his raven hair become filled with silver-grey tufts? Did he have hair? Our curiosity knew no end. We began to squint through the dimly lit roads, hoping to catch sight of a person we hadn't seen in years.

Suddenly, he appeared around the bend farthest from us. I still remember his tall figure and the nonchalant way he'd walk down the road. The amber streetlights fell smoothly across his face, giving him a golden bronze look. A happy smile curved my lips and Gina's. We'd sacrificed the money from our summer jobs to pay someone to take us to his house. We wore our finest apparel and couldn't wait for him to compliment us. Maybe he'd even share a couple of stories with us! Who knew?

He drew nearer and nearer. His eyes met mine first, and instantly, he froze. I smiled, and just as I opened my mouth to call out to him, he did the unexpected. He spun around on his heels and began to head in the opposite direction—towards the dark side of the road. His legs moved very quickly, and it seemed as if he'd been injected with adrenaline. Puzzled, I began to run after him. Had he not seen us? Gina ran just as fast, with her footsteps echoing beside mine.

We split up. I went one way, and Gina went the other. We were to meet somewhere in the middle. We ran until our legs grew weak and our lungs hurt. We searched every corner and even risked checking the dark woods that lined the roads. I'd called out to my father in the darkness, trying hard to blink away the tears that stung my eyes. The only response that greeted me was the song of the crickets. Somehow, amid my growing fatigue, I realized our father had avoided us.

He didn't want to see us.

We've all heard the words, "You have to forgive." Still, most people do not understand that these words are a door. This door reveals a hidden passage that is a hundred meters deep, two hundred meters wide, and a thousand meters long, and the whole mystery doesn't end there. It extends down the passageways, creating a nasty labyrinth that could have the best puzzlers confused.

Going down the passageways myself, I have realized that, sometimes, the guides and maps for the labyrinth may have to be self-sourced. The traveler on the path of forgiveness must be ready to stir up the nastiest concoctions and recipes using raw materials from the heart, mind, and soul. These words and definitions should impose a simple task, but no, forgiveness may be just as hard as reducing Mount Everest into small rocky crumbles.

Let us explore my experience. As a little girl, I learned one of the harshest theories about life. Although both sides of my grandparents remained married until death parted them, absentee fathers were normal in my family history. I would not see my father for long periods of time. No, my dad was not in the prison system, nor was he off serving his country in the military. Instead, he was in his own world of alcohol, ostracized from our world by his choice of beverage and choice of friends. My "father hunger" was never filled until I was in my forties.

I got used to living that way, having a periodic father. In exchange, I expected him to at least compensate for that by spending more time with us when he was sober.

But, as I waited for that payday to come, my mother presented him with two options. He had to give up drinking and be with the family or choose his drinks and cut ties with us.

I expected him to choose the former. At least, he did owe us that much. He owed us an apology for staying distant. He owed us an apology for causing us to wait for him to become sober so we could have a relationship. I believed alcohol could never have so much effect on him that he'd forsake his own family. I thought that he loved and cherished us even more than his drinks.

If you have been paying attention, you will soon realize that I loved him. Understanding what love is may be crucial to understanding my plight. So, yes, let us tackle that first.

WHAT IS LOVE?

Understanding what love was to a young child like me might not be easy. Might you ponder this question? What did I have going on in my head? Funny enough, I did not even know the theoretical definitions of love. Mine came as a natural inclination. I had an undying affection for my dad. So, I could smile and laugh with him, even when I knew he would not remember the conversation. I ached for the times he was sober. I yearned for the times he came to our school to visit us.

Regardless of how dark or ugly his other side was, I still loved him. Nothing may ever be purer than the love of a child. It is one of the most genuine emotions ever gracing the earth. And once that love is lost, it may never be regained.

Now that you know what love meant to me, I would like to shed light on what heartbreak felt like. No child should ever have to know what heartbreak is. Most times, when kids like me suffer from the adverse effects of heartbreak, their hearts are broken by their parents first.

My heart shattered into a million pieces when I realized my dad wasn't coming back to live with us. I remember how shocked I was. How could he choose a life we were not a part of? We were the fundamental entities in his life, and he made it look like we meant absolutely nothing to him.

At three years old, I remember being angry, sad, and alone without him. Anger's climbing tendrils began to shroud the surface of my heart very quickly. I was so young then. These emotions almost suffocated me. I did not know how to manage that. I was hurt and disappointed. I had not expected that anyone would ever disappoint me. Life was supposed to be nothing but a bed of roses.

He visited a couple of times, and I tried to feed myself with a bit of hope. Maybe he would realize his mistakes, apologize, and come home. Then, at the age of six, all my hope crumbled. He had come to our school to visit us during recess. Gina and I were one grade apart and had recess together. She said, "Hey Cassie, there is dad." We raced to him. We embraced and talked until the break ended. He never came again.

Years passed before I ever saw him again. He never showed up for birthdays or holidays. Honestly, I do not remember him calling to ask about our well-being either. But I loved him. There is something intense about that genuine kind of love. It does not get suffocated easily. It never died, even though I convinced myself that I was better off without an alcoholic dad.

Longing for that love, Gina and I went to our grandmother's house. My dad moved in with her after our grandfather passed away in 1981. As teenagers, she and I worked summer jobs with the Davy Crockett Forestry Service. We saved enough money to purchase our first car together -a 1979 burgundy Chevrolet Chevette. We were excited about the vehicle with the automatic gear shift between the two front seats rather than on the steering wheel. Ironically, neither of us had a driver's license, no car insurance, and our dad lived twenty-five miles away.

Gina was more experienced at driving than I was. Our Aunt Mary gave us driving lessons using her car. I would sit in the back seat and Gina in the front as she taught us how to drive. After a while, Aunt Mary trusted Gina to drive her car to the store, which was four miles on the main highway from our house. Once the confidence was met, we stepped out on our adventure in our car to see our dad. I still hoped he'd be willing to come back. In that same vein, I waited for him. The rest of the story, you already know.

I disregarded him thickly from then on. Thinking about him gave me a nasty spread of goosebumps, and I constantly tried hard to detach him from my daily thoughts. In my opinion, he did not deserve a place in my heart or mind—these things tortured my heart, mind, and soul. Thoughts of him would randomly flow into my head, and I would have to remind myself again of his choice. I held resentment against him as big as Texas. I did not see him as my father. I know this is ugly and sad, but true. I saw him as a sperm donor. Sometimes, the ideas would come so strongly I would cry my eyes out.

I became a mess: a holy mess filled with bitterness.

Whenever I considered how much I had to struggle with my feelings, I would hate him more. Every time I thought of how he would force us to live a life where he wasn't in, I'd conclude in my heart that he wasn't worth my forgiveness. Another thing you should note is how dark my heart was becoming. I was learning to deal with my love for him the hard way, and for some reason, it worked.

The anger pushed me to live my life to the best of my ability. I felt the constant need to prove to him that he was not needed. I wanted to become a woman who would show her father how much of a great person she turned out to be. Life became too much of a competition, and really, such unhealthy themes sabotaged my mind. Come what may, the thoughts of revenge made it too hard to stop. I disregarded having myself wrecked in a bid to prove my point to him.

Is it easy for you to take the side of this young teenager? You would agree that she was indeed wronged. She did not in any way deserve what her father threw her way. She did not deserve to shun all of the fun of having a dad around and then chase after an unhealthy way of living.

I always convinced myself of these things too. I was not wrong at all. I believed anyone who tried to counter my opinions was just some fool who did not understand what it meant to have their heart broken as a kid. Perhaps I found some strange kind of comfort or security in that. Who knows.

There is a scenario closely similar to mine I want to share. You might have heard the story countless times, but I'll tell it again. A supreme being with power, riches, and everything you could imagine was king of all things

—the Alpha and Omega. Angels would bow to his feet, and a thousand and one elders would sing his praises. His home illuminates the finest treasures and materials. Simply put, he lacked nothing.

One fateful day, he felt compelled to act on one of his long-time thoughts. He was a powerful being that the other beings he had created could not compare. Something about the aura he exuded seemed more significant than what the beings could contend. He felt a desire for fellowship to some extent. He thought of creating an entity that could stay right by his side and commune with him daily. He wanted a genuine relationship. Colossians 1:16b (ESV) echoes the point: "All things were created through him and for him."

In that manner, he created an entity that looked like him and named him "man." He gave him all he needed, and his love was so deep for his creation. Regularly, in the cool of the day, he would leave his glorious place of abode to dwell with beings molded out of clay. His acts appeared ridiculous to the angels and other beings that had existed aforetime. What could "man" possibly be that he would leave all for him?

Now, this man and this powerful being grew very close. They laughed together, talked together, and even exchanged secrets. Finally, the powerful being gave his friend an instruction and expected him to obey it. The man did just what the powerful being had instructed him not to do. On realizing what man had done, the powerful being became disappointed and angry. Why would his friend go against him?

The betrayal caused a rift between them and could have possibly severed their friendship. In defiance, the negative actions of the man continued, but the love the being had for him remained constant. Now, I would like you to take a bit of a drift to consider this story. Yes, it is a real story that happened at the beginning of time. The powerful being was God, and his friend was "man."

The first time I heard it, I was perplexed. How did God not get angry with the man yet continue to love the man? He could have hated him for his actions, but then and even today, we still know of his great love for man. God sent his only begotten son to die for the same people He had great reason to hate. Why? What was the mystery of his love?

How could I have still loved my father and given him a chance after all he had done to me? Was that even possible for me? How could I let go of the pain and disappointment just to reach out to him again? How could I make the past drizzle away as if it had never happened? Why not forgive? Did I have to be like God? Why do I have to do what God did? You would believe I had a right to my emotions. I had a right to be me.

Yes?

Over the years, I have discovered the vainness in such a way of living, and here, I will reveal my findings to you.

CHAPTER 2
The Christian Life

Understanding the principles of forgiveness is almost impossible unless light is shed on the Christian life. The Christian life is a life guided by God's precepts. A Christian displays Christ-like attributes. We can find these attributes by spending time with God and His word.

Let us relate to what happened at Antioch in the book of Acts.

"...and when he (Barnabas) found him (Saul), he brought him to Antioch. So, for a whole year, Barnabas and Saul met with the church and taught great numbers of people. The disciples were called Christians first at Antioch." Acts 11:26 NIV (emphasis added)

It is uncertain if the believers called themselves Christian or if their enemies tagged them out of spite. Either way, they belonged to Christ.

What can we tag as the attributes of Christ? What traits did the unbelievers see in the believers that moved them so strongly that they had to come up with a name for them? Let us go a little further.

"For the fruit of the Spirit is love, joy, peace, longsuffering, gentleness, goodness, faith, meekness, temperance: against such, there is no law." Galatians 5:22, 23 KJV

These attributes demonstrate characteristics the Christians displayed then and now. If we looked more deeply, we would see that all of them require a forgiving spirit. What makes these attributes so inherent is that it is impossible to wield without the presence of the Spirit inside you. "For the fruit of the Spirit is..." Yet, human flesh is prone to all sorts of emotions—anger, malice, hatred, selfishness, jealousy, and discord. If you tried to overcome these negative feelings on your own, you would get frustrated repeatedly.

I have known of the Lord since I was five years old. The first scripture I learned in Sunday School was "God is Love." My Sunday school teacher Mrs. Guice and the eight Sunday school kids were nestled in the far-left corner of the sanctuary, adjacent to the pulpit. Sitting on the dark brown church pews, you could hear the screech in the wood when we got up or sat down.

I sat in the middle or sometimes on the far-left end of the row. Mrs. Guice would pull out a 4" x 6" card with a

Bible story printed on it. She would ask each of us to stand beside her as she sat in her chair. One by one we read from that card as she helped us pronounce the more complicated words.

After everyone finished their part, Mrs. Guice would explain and elaborate on the Bible story. At the end of class, she asked, "What did you learn in Sunday school class today?" When my turn came, I answered, "God is love." I can say that was my introduction to God. At five years old, I did not fully understand what that meant. It was many years before I fully understood that verse.

I found it easy to harbor negative thoughts and saw nothing wrong in keeping a grudge. But, after a while, I noticed I struggled to achieve closure. I wanted to be that perfect woman with no issues at all. So, I tried to fight against the bitter emotions that accumulated within me. I failed miserably.

How do you overcome such a pattern and not let it lord over your life?

First, you need to recognize that you need help. A failure to do so is one of the first signs that you have a problem. The fruits of the Spirit listed above are yardsticks you can use to realize your state. The Bible explains that people are known by the fruits they bear. Once you notice that love, joy, peace, longsuffering, and all other necessary virtues are lacking, consider it time to seek healing.

In acknowledging your frame of mind, realize that your life is against God's principles. It is not wise to be against God. The more a person stays out of sync with God, the more he denies himself certain possibilities and gifts.

God hates an unforgiving spirit. He wants us to be like him in all areas of our lives. He desires that we forgive people of their transgressions against us—no matter how grievous—since he has also forgiven us of ours.

My first issue was feeling justified in not forgiving my dad. I also wasn't considering God's emotions which made it easy for me to keep up with that act. I did not recognize he expected much more from me. I even got angry at someone else for having almost the same attitude I had.

Because God loves us dearly, we may hurt him deeply by choosing not to fellowship with him. Recall, God created man primarily for fellowship. He wanted people with whom he could talk and relate. By choosing to remain in an unforgiving state we push him away. Ponder this thought. How does God feel to see the very people he sacrificed so much for belittling his importance in their lives?

Every time we fail to acknowledge God, we tell him we do not need him. Let us put ourselves in God's shoes for a second. Yes, just a second. How hurtful is that?

How much devastation have we imposed on him? While we are harboring grudges, hate, malice, jealousy, and unforgiveness against someone else, we are simultaneously doing the same thing.

What difference exists between us and those who are now at war with God? Answering this question will go a long way in helping you understand. Also, plotting out a graph of how little you grow while harboring negative traits will give you an extensive look at where you are and how much farther you must go.

The prophet Haggai noted:

> Now this is what the Lord Almighty says: "Give careful thought to your ways. You have planted much, but harvested little. You eat, but never have enough. You drink, but never have your fill. You put on clothes, but are not warm. You earn wages, only to put them in a purse with holes in it.
> This is what the Lord Almighty says: "Give careful thought to your ways. Haggai 1: 5-7 NIV

Consider your ways carefully if you never achieve a sense of fulfillment in any area of your life. We can be busy doing a whole lot of things, good things. But when we go home and look in the mirror in the quiet times of night, do we smile and exhale, or do we each shake our head from side to side and wonder why am I feeling so unsettled?

I celebrate New Year's Day twice a year, on January 1st, then, again, on my birthday in September. I sit down, put pen to paper, and evaluate where I am and where I'm going. I look at all aspects of where I am physically (Am I taking care of my body?), psychologically (Am I taking care of my mind and emotions?), spiritually (Am I right with God from His perspective?), financially (Is there balance?), and relationally (What is toxic and what is not?). The inventory of my life allows me to see if there is still something that remains to be settled.

Every time, the checkbox for every other facet of my life would be filled with a tick and penned-in suggestions. But something in the spiritual box was unchecked. The word "forgive" would pop up, and I would grow frustrated. What did that mean? I never could boast of achieving a hundred percent score; of course not. I could not boast of wholeness or a perfectly planned life.

The words of God, above, serve as a calling to us. If you are struggling so hard or finding no sense of satisfaction no matter what you do, you need to look back and see where you went wrong. It's not always other people, though we try to point the guilty stick in their direction.

It is at this point most people discover the bitterness in their own hearts.

When I considered my life's path, I traced my struggles to the bitterness in my heart. Out of that bitterness had come anger, dislike, malice, strife, and everything that was not right. At this point, I began to realize that my ways were wrong. Not forgiving my father had led to me gaining little to no satisfaction from anything else.

Maybe you have suffered setbacks because you have not forgiven the person who hurt you. Yes, you might have felt a searing pain, but you can set yourself free! You, too, can break down the impediments that bitterness has placed in your way. Tell yourself firmly that you need to move forward. You need to laugh genuinely again. You need to breathe freely again!

See the beautiful life you could have if you did not hold the grudge, and then yearn for it. Desire is one of the most potent tools for pushing anyone into actualizing a plan. For instance, when you desire a cake, you look for ways to get it, even if the bakery is not nearby. I know someone who drives thirty minutes from their house to get a Starbucks coffee. You may be the kind of person who hates going out, or even getting dressed, for such things, but because of your desire, you look past the inconvenience and head out.

Head out now!

- Ask for forgiveness
- Repent, change your heart, change your ways
- Forgive others

The first step in the process is to ask God for forgiveness. I realized how much I had pushed God away by harboring so many bad feelings and emotions. Here is something profound that I learned, and please take note; although I kept God at arm's length—knowingly or unknowingly—he still stayed with me.

How do I know this? How can I prove that God never forsook me? Joshua 1:5 made this point clear when God said he would never leave or forsake us. God never lies! When God made that statement, he never said its validity was tied to anything. He chose to stay with me no matter what I did. And he will stay with you.

"so is my word that goes out from my mouth: It will not return to me empty, but will accomplish what I desire and achieve the purpose for which I sent it." Isaiah 55:11 NIV

God could have chosen to vent his anger at me. He could have decided to take my breath away. But he protected and provided for me. His love sustained my life. The only issue was that my lack of a forgiving spirit hindered God from doing more.

The only plans God thinks of for us are tailored toward our good. He only desires that we reach an expected end. By harboring ill feelings toward my father, I prevented God from being able to act upon his words.

After realizing these things, the next step is to reach out to God. God understands virtually all that we present to him. So, it is not wrong to cry your eyes out and tell him how much you are hurting. It's not wrong to tell him how much frustration and struggle you have been through as a result. Honestly, you can tell God that you do not want to forgive another. Now, this does not mean you do not forgive or refuse to do what's right. But you can go to God and pour out your true feelings. He will hear you and understand.

It is not wrong to express to him that the pain was so great it almost swallowed you up. One of the very reasons the portal of heaven opened, and Jesus came right into this earth was that he wanted to pass through everything man could ever pass through. That way, Jesus would know the perfect way of consoling all that came to him. So, yes, God has the key you need to unlock your heart from its prison! He has the key to getting rid of the void in your heart.

Once you have poured out your heart to God, you can continue to explain your findings. It is not wrong to say that the bitterness has spurred anger, hate, malice, and everything God doesn't like. Confessing those truths to him is the first way to open your heart. You acknowledge to God that you know those things were wrong, and you are genuinely sorry for them.

When I apologized to God that same way, my anger did not go away instantly. This is where the word of God comes in. The Bible explains that the word of God plays the function of renewing our minds and giving us a total transformation. So, the more I pondered God's word, the easier it became to forgive. The best way to solve a problem is by exposing it to the word of God.

- **Accept the help of his Spirit and then acknowledge the power of his word.**

One way God helps us overcome our angry emotions is by giving us his Spirit. The Holy Spirit can ease our pain and stress. The Holy Spirit makes it much more possible to live the kind of life God envisions his children living. The Spirit guides you into all truths and helps you live up to God's expectations. The Spirit is the one that helps you meditate on the Word, so that the negative thinking and intense feelings of dislike, or hate, can melt into nothing.

Before I knew the Lord, I mean really knew the Lord, I considered it impossible to forgive my father. My heart was set in stone, and my decision was made. Up to that point in my life, I had lived with the pain of the past. I did not see my father coming to apologize to me, and I also didn't see myself going to make peace with him. After all, I was not in any way wrong. He was the one who left. I was the child. He was the adult. He was the one who had done wrong. He was the one who needed to make his ways right.

Do you see the blame game coming into play here? The Holy Spirit's first act was to bring me realization of that mindset. One thing about the Holy Spirit is that he will never take the side of anyone when it comes to an issue. Whether you are mistaken or correct, he will look right at you as the one who is responsible for change. He will try to make you understand what you can do to make things better. Living the Christian life is all about choosing to be different! It is this difference that tags believers as Christians.

- **Repent. Change your heart, change your ways.**

Notice how God sits as a refiner in Malachi 3:2-3 ESV

> ...*For he is like a refiner's fire and a fuller's soap: And he shall sit as a refiner and purifier of silver, purify the sons of Levi, and refine them as gold and silver that they may offer unto the Lord an offering in righteousness.*

Our time with God is fitted to this purpose. God refines us so much that we find it undemanding to forgive. No one wants to admit they are wrong, but remember, repentance is not an option. We are being refined. As such, we find that as our heart begins to change, our ways will follow suit.

If you have ever wondered how bitterness, shame, guilt, unforgiveness, or any other negative thing you are dealing with in your heart, will ever leave, I recommend you submit to the Lord. Believe that only he can rescue you from the fire of negative emotions eating away at you. Every time it gets hard for you, confidently submit to him. Pour out all your cares and worries on him. He always has a way out of every mess we find ourselves in.

It does not matter if you have kept a grudge or harbored negative emotions for months or years. He is capable. "He is faithful and just and will forgive us our sins and purify us from all unrighteousness." 1 John 1:9 NIV The mechanics of how that process comes to be should not be any of our business. Once again, we are being refined.

All we should focus on getting is the result of what we asked of him. More simply, the Amplified version says it this way:

> *If we {freely} admit that we have sinned*
> *and confess our sins, He is faithful and*

just {true to His own nature and promises}, and will forgive our sins and cleanse us continually from all unrighteousness {our wrongdoing, everything not in conformity with His will and purpose}.

- **Yield yourself to forgiveness.**

"Then came Peter to him and said, 'Lord, how often should I forgive someone who sins against me? Seven times?' 'No, not seven times,' Jesus replied, 'but seventy times seven!'" Matthew 18:21 NLT

Living the Christian life means being willing and ready to forgive as often as possible. I have often wondered whether this seemed accurate or fair. We are giving so much and receiving little (if anything) from the person that wounded us.

Recently, I received a phone call from a sister-friend. I'll call her Angie. We met over fifteen years ago at a church my family and I visited and later became members of. She was a nurse, and we found common interest as I had been in the medical field while serving in the military.

"Hey, Sis, how are you?" She greeted me. I could hear her smile through the phone. The small chat began, as you can imagine when two women get together. Suddenly, there was a pause. "Sis, I need your advice."

Angie sounded firm, but I noticed a hint of anticipation to her voice as she spoke. I was at my desk working through the mad rush of emails accumulated over my two days of rest. I sat up in my chair and replied, "Okay, Sis go ahead. Tell me what's going on."

"Our Women's Empowerment Leadership is having a conference, and I am one of the speakers. Our topic is 'Rekindling Relationships'. May I share with you something I've never told you? This is also what I'm going to share when I speak at the conference."

I did not want to interrupt her but wanted her to know I was paying attention. "Yes, Sis, I'm listening."

"My husband and I divorced for a time and remarried." She exhaled, paused, then continued.

"Our problems started with verbal arguing then became physical abuse. I remember his fist would meet my face. The blow was so hard I could not go to work, so I'd call in. I made up excuses for the bruises on my body. I tried drinking alcohol and smoking marijuana to numb the pain—it did not work.

The physical battery played out in the bedroom. He positioned me in a way that caused me pain and suffering. Night after night, it became evident I couldn't survive this. I felt I wasn't fit to care for my kids. I had become a beaten, battered, broken woman."

My mind could not picture such a thing about my dear friend. I listened on.

"I was so close to losing my mind. I felt so worthless. I thought, if the trauma of being beaten didn't kill me, I'd eventually kill myself; at least I'd be out of this mess!

I sought counseling. I cried out to God, and I asked Him to help me survive this. If He would just get me out of this tumultuous relationship, I would serve Him all the days of my life!

We divorced."

Although Angie was released from that relationship, her low self-esteem made its bed in her mind. I thought how Angie, deprived of the true pleasures of marriage, having the weight of her position as a nurse, and yearning for a pain-free life, had fought the siren call of suicide. I wept for my friend.

She continued.

"After my divorce, I fell prey to some of the most dangerous relationships--the kind most women don't usually survive. For example, I became involved with a man who worked for the Texas Department of Criminal Justice. He was previously married with children from that marriage."

I could sense her anxiety as she conveyed her story. I imagined her fantasizing, "This is the one. We will marry and live 'happily ever after'." Perhaps she felt I would judge her when she told me she thought he loved her. Maybe embarrassment swept over her, when she revealed she became pregnant and had a baby out of wedlock.

This is what she told me next.

"The devil had sent a man into my life who was a functional alcoholic. Numbing himself to life's existence, he would drown himself in alcohol in the presence of my children and me. He hid his weed (marijuana) at my house. He remained either drunk or high.

Not only was he an alcoholic, but he was also an ex-con who served several years in prison for assault and battery, theft, and drug distribution—yeah!!! That was what I was dealing with!

Unforgiveness, anger, hurt, bitterness, trauma from beatings, sexual abuse, and layers of negative emotions burdened me."

Talk about low self-esteem. I heard her sniffle and try to swallow the clump in her throat. I imagined she bowed her head in shame, concerned I would think less of her. I had so much compassion for Angie. I had grown up seeing other women go down the same path. Some grew stronger and got out of the toxic relationship. Others stayed, believing that was their only choice. Still, others, like my Aunt Josephine, had not survived.

"I'm sorry you went through that, Sister. My heart aches for you," I responded.

"This guy introduced me to drugs. I graduated with my nursing degree and worked at a local hospital. When the time came for the drug screening, I knew I wouldn't pass. My boyfriend supplied me with a substance that cleansed the urine. It worked, and I passed the drug test.

The level and intensity of the abuse this guy would use to break me down had me almost walking away from my calling as a nurse. He violated every open area on my body. I literally felt myself sinking into a dark hole. It was hell at a high price. A price I simply could not pay!

I fell to my knees and cried out to my Heavenly Father with tears that I believed touched the throne of heaven!"

Angie didn't just weep for that situation; she also wept in grief. Her mother, sister, Dad, and brother passed away during that time. She felt alone. God heard her. He strategically placed people and a church in her path to love on her and her now three children. She then took a fifteen-year sabbatical from inappropriate relationships.

"I grew spiritually and became stronger and wiser. I began to seek God's purpose for my life. He revealed it. I listened and began the work."

The first thing Angie did was ask God to forgive her. Next, she forgave herself. God worked on her heart. Not only that, God worked on her ex-husband's heart. They were willing to ask and receive forgiveness from each other. They reunited in marriage and are married to this day.

If forgiveness were not so important in our lives as Christians, God would not have written the words. Jesus did not specify the kinds of offense we are to forgive. Forgive if it is the vilest of crimes or slander. And when forgiveness seems complicated, remember, you and I are not perfect people, so we have no right to withhold our forgiveness.

Not forgiving others places you on the wrong side with God, and because you value God's acceptance so much, why not forgive? Choose to do what is right. It would be hard to ignore a cheating wife or husband. It would be hard to forgive someone who violated or abused you. That is why our need for the Holy Spirit can never be underrated.

The Spirit of God helps us to become slow to anger. Anger is not destructive. On the contrary, anger is a natural healthy emotion. It's the actions of being angry that cause the negative. What harms us is succumbing to the anger so much that we allow it to push us into a deep dark place.

Being in that place, for even a moment, may cause us a lifetime of suffering. When you are angry, acknowledge it to yourself. Pause. Ask God to help you be resilient against the antagonistic force. In response, God will enable you to become stronger and have a healthy temperance.

Angie was determined to be a person God delights in. Being able to forgive came quickly after that.

CHAPTER 3
Speak Your Hurt

We often find ourselves in scenarios where it is almost impossible to forgive people for crimes they commit against us. Crime may seem like a strong word, but if you ask the person on the receiving end, "crime" does describe the offense.

Rena was a tranquil girl but outgoing when she needed to be. She was active in sports and loved being involved in church. The time came for the youth to fellowship at another church. Rena was excited about the chance to get away from home, even if it was only for the day.

The ride to the new church was filled with chatter and laughter among the group of teenagers. Rena delighted in the different atmosphere and activities other youth were a part of. Finally, the festivities were over, and it was time to go home. Unfortunately, the adults had decided to alter their route home. Rena was left riding home alone with the pastor.

When he went inside the church to get his briefcase, Rena stayed outside. An awkward feeling told her not to go back in. When the pastor came out, she got in the passenger side of his truck and pressed against the door. Any more force, she thought, would have made her concerns too apparent.

"You could have come into the church," he said, "I wasn't going to kiss you." The look and smile on his face were enough to make Rena want to jump out of the moving truck. She looked straight ahead and was quiet as a mouse. She thought of when he had put his arms around her waist and patted her on her backside. He made it look so innocent in front of other church members. They had thought nothing of it, or, at least, no one had said anything if they did.

"Will you be my girlfriend?" he had asked mellowly. She was seventeen years old, but had enough sense to say 'No,' and she did. He told her of his impressive business and financial status. She knew he was married and had children. Also, he and one of the ladies at the church often kept company together. She could not believe this was happening, but it was happening to her.

Rena stared at the road and the trees passing by. "Just take me home, please," she responded. That was the first and last time she was alone with this man. He was her pastor, the Shepherd of a church. He was married with children and a participant in adultery. How hard is that to forgive?

We try to justify ourselves with thoughts that such people do not deserve forgiveness to begin with. This may work out initially, but eventually, such justification only settles an incredible discomfort within us. Since we cannot forget them, the next time we see them, we find ourselves shooting them hot glares of disgust. From my experience, that approach always cultivates the ground of our hearts for hatred.

Whether we like it or not, people will always find a way to infuriate us. For most of those people, an apology never enters their thoughts. It is up to us to free our minds from this anger and the gut-wrenching tears that resonate inside us.

The first thing to do is to choose to forgive on purpose. Why not forgive? Forgiving can be like one of those big "horse" pills the doctor prescribes for pain. The doctor instructs you not to break it up but to swallow it whole. No matter how much water you drink, the pill has a way of sticking in your throat. You swallow and swallow eventually getting it down, only to taste the residue on your tongue.

When you genuinely forgive a person, you find a safe way to unhinge your mind from your angry thoughts. Yes, the residue of pain is there, but you prevent the build-up of hate and unhealthy anger. However, the process is not as easy as it sounds. Let us see how to go about it.

- **Understand your primary purpose in life**

Knowing the reason for your existence will guide you in understanding how to live and act. You know you have a vital goal ahead of you and cannot afford to get distracted or infected with unhealthy thoughts. You must preserve your mind's health.

Getting back to my own story. Remember my inability to forgive my father affected me? Every time I tried to achieve closure and balance, I'd remember my father and get frustrated all over again. Every time I felt this frustration, I'd find myself detesting him all the more.

What was my goal?

Was struggling and hating a person worth the damage it did to my life?

What things were suffered as a result?

What things had I missed out on?

How much farther along in life could I have been if I had forgiven him?

We should ask ourselves the tough questions when we find it hard to bring ourselves to the point of forgiving people that offend us. In the second story I shared from the first chapter, I focused on God creating us for companionship. With no boundaries, God wanted man to fellowship with him. But that connection was severed when man heard the voice of sin louder than the voice of God.

Disobedience, lack of forgiveness, and lack of self-control all keep us farther away from God. As a result, we find it hard to commune with him, and in the process, lose our bearing, directions, and focus. A person's life will never attain balance if God is not in it.

From my teenage years into adulthood, I restricted God by bearing a grudge against my father. Did I notice the effect of this restriction? Yes, I did. I got frustrated a million times and found it hard to find closure. Yet, at first, I still felt the need to justify myself. I did not see myself doing any wrong by not forgiving my father. After all, he did not deserve forgiveness; so, I thought.

I always asked myself, "Why should I forgive? I tried over and over again, but nothing ever stuck. Yet, God is very gracious and began to shed his light on my life. He helped me understand that things would only improve when I forgave my dad and those who hurt me. I needed to allow God to do what he wanted to do in me to reach my full potential. This process is what I would describe as getting rid of the one last boundary between God and me.

If we are not living up to God's first purpose of creating us—companionship—then it's safe to say we have botched our first essence in life. The one reason we should prioritize fellowship with God is this—it controls every other part of life. In the presence of God, we find direction and our other secondary purposes. A person who does not forgive may end up like the hamster running in circles on the wheel, which means not going anywhere.

- **Understand the effect of forgiveness on your brain and health**

The heart and brain are the central areas that control forgiveness. Resentment consumes the heart of one who does not forgive. It takes all the space and suffocates you. You can't freely think, laugh, or even hear God's voice. It is like a prison, forming a wall around you, blocking you from many realities and possibilities.

In the article "The Neurobiology of Forgiveness", Dr. Heidi Moawad writes:

> "Forgiveness is a change in mental state in which a person decides and succeeds in eliminating anger toward another person who has deliberately done something unfair or harmful to them.

Forgiveness means that a person is aware of injustice and has to make a decision to release blame or anger."

William Park is a writer and editor for BBC based in London, UK. He writes on various subjects such as health, occupational and social psychology, and culture. He shared about an exchange partnership. In this partnership, we exchange our stress, risk of heart disease, mental illness, success and longer, happier life for three words: "I forgive you".

Park also quotes Loren Toussaint, a psychologist who studies forgiveness at Luther College, Iowa who expressed, "I don't know if there is a sphere of your life that will not be positively impacted by being more forgiving."

The past affects your present, and it is assured to control your future if things aren't put in their rightful place. When you forgive someone, it does not mean that you have forgotten what they have done. Instead, forgiveness puts you in the driver's seat to press the gas and move on.

Don't look back in the mirror to unforgiveness. Don't let it define you any longer. Rather, rewire your brain to unleash love and kindness. Focus on who you are today and what defines you now. Letting go allows those around you, and yourself, to enjoy present perceptions not colored by past perspectives.

- **Understand the effect forgiveness could have on your social life**

You need to know that an unforgiving spirit stunts the growth of your social life. When you are friends with someone, there will be a time when your ideas and interests clash, which may result in a fight. The fight may result in a terrible scenario where you find it hard to forgive. Once you refuse to forgive one person, you find it easy not to forgive the second and third person.

Everybody wants to find a person who genuinely cares for them. We all want friends, but have we bothered to consider the traits that attract friends? How open are you? Has the state of your heart closed you off from the world? Has it made you see no hope in relationships? Has it made you decide that everyone is the same? If you have incorporated such attitudes into your mindset, you should work hard to eliminate them.

Do not allow past betrayals to keep you from new relationships. True friendship happens when two people help each other get better. Proverbs 27:17 explains it as iron sharpening iron. People rub off on each other their values, beliefs, and principles. You deserve to have a true friend. You deserve to go on picnics, dates, and all that fun stuff people do to hang out with those they love. Do not let your inability to forgive steal that from you!

I have discovered that harboring a grudge can be very consuming. It takes up space in your heart, clouds your mind, eats at your soul, and robs you of your time. You may spend so much time trying to contain and struggle with your feelings that you find it hard to see the need for anything else. So, you go about with a frown plastered to your face or a rigid body.

You do not realize the atmosphere you are creating makes life unpleasant for others. Pastor Jimmy and Karen Evans founded a ministry called *Marriage Today*. During one of their marriage seminars, he talked about how Karen went about the day with a "sour look on her face." No one wants to get close to someone who is always frowning.

This look stemmed from an argument they had several days before about Jimmy always going to play golf and not spending quality time at home. Karen felt hurt and unheard. Jimmy thought she was just nagging. He ignored her feelings and went on about his days. Neither had any nice words to offer.

Then, one day, this old hurt catapulted into a big argument, and Karen left the room crying. Jimmy felt divorce was imminent. But he loved Karen and did not want a divorce. In the moment's stillness, Jimmy realized there had been much hurt and pain in the marriage. He found Karen still crying. As quick as a heartbeat, forgiveness sprouted from the depths of the dirt. Jimmy apologized for disregarding Karen's feelings and devaluing her and what she added to the marriage and family. Karen also apologized for her passivity and for not acknowledging that Jimmy needed an outlet.

So why not forgive?

Maybe you have been wondering why people are not inclined to be friends with you. No, do not think of yourself as toxic or unpitying. But, would it help if you got rid of the veil that prevents people from seeing the real jovial you? Pluck out the hate in your heart so you can live freely and laugh freely. Get rid of the sour onions and embrace life again. You have great skills and talents that make people want to get closer to you. Do not push them away with a bitter heart.

You can't afford to lose people who could be valuable to your life and future!

You cannot afford to lose relationships that could help you grow into a better you!

If you are confused about what to do, try this. Speak up! Be intentional in letting people know what they said or did hurt you. Such declarations will keep you in communication with others. Let them know your struggles if you trust them with your intimate feelings. So often, God uses those very same people to help promote healing in his children.

Sonia and I met at a church I attended in Conroe, Texas. She is the director of The Legacy Center, a non-profit, faith-based discipleship and recovery home for women. I was a Lead Sunday school teacher, and Sonia and some of the ladies in the program attended the class. One Sunday before class started, Sonia asked if I could speak with her after class. Of course, I said, "Yes."

She spoke passionately about her organization and what it offers women and their children who are in the program. "I wanted to ask," she said, "Would you be interested in teaching a Bible class one day a week or possibly be a mentor to the ladies?" She added, "I enjoy how you teach the Sunday school class, and I think your personal story will benefit the ladies." I spoke about my reluctance to forgive my father during an earlier class.

I felt honored and excited. What an opportunity to empower the lives of women. However, I didn't want to answer too quickly because I have a husband and three active children at home. I told her I would give her an answer on Wednesday. When Wednesday came, the answer was "Yes."

Legacy already had a curriculum, but Sonia told me,

"Whatever God tells you to teach, do that." I felt honored, but then I thought, what will I teach?" I prayed. God answered. I taught from the book *The Search for Significance*, by Robert S. McGee. This book had impacted my life, by freeing me from a "people-pleasing" mindset and encouraging me to let go of the pain of the past.

A member of the class, I will call Sally, had lived in the trauma of her past, being homeless with two children and going through withdrawal from drug abuse. When she was introduced to the Legacy Program, her initial hesitation caused her to delay attending for several weeks. Sally could not believe the people at Legacy, let alone anyone else, could love her without wanting to take something from her.

I challenged Sally and the other participants during class to look at themselves in the mirror. Not as they looked to put on make-up or remove it, but to look deep into their own eyes to see their soul. This seeing of your soul is relevant to your self-worth and your identity. The Legacy ladies responded positively to the teaching. Self-forgiveness took place in that classroom.

Sally graduated from the nine-month program and continued as an intern, working on her life and being a good mother. She continues to connect with me several times a year. She reminisces about the class days and how that teaching opened her eyes to her own self-worth, leading her to better things in her future. Our pains of the past were similar.

Not only was I in their presence to help them, but our relationship also freed me from something I had thought I was over. I volunteered with Legacy for five years and would have continued had I not moved away. I taught various studies, mentored, and spent quality time with ladies I saw as my older sisters, younger sisters, and nieces. I carry Legacy in my heart, praying for the healing and freedom of every soul entering the program.

The last thing I need to place under this section for you may seem too unrealistic and impossible. Please don't close the book on me. Sometimes, the person you hold a grudge against might just be the one you need. He or she may be the very person who will lead you into the paths of success and fulfillment.

You have heard the saying, "Don't burn a bridge" because you may need that same bridge to get to the other side (of hope, peace, freedom, success, etc.). Yet, some bridges should be burned. Explore the facts and use discernment in the actions you take.

- **Understand that the person you cannot forgive may need your help**

Self-denying, generous, and altruistic are words that define selflessness. It is an attitude that describes putting other people first and yourself next. Selflessness helped me immensely in forgiving my father. It caused me to see him differently. No one turns to alcohol because they want to. They are trying to numb the pain. Most people believe they forget all their sorrows by drowning themselves in alcohol or other substances. But, of course, once they are sober, all the problems still remain.

Why should we get angry at such people?

What if they need someone to reach out to them? What if they need a little bit of comfort? Should I choose not to forgive my father if his addiction resulted from his sorrows taking a toll on him? My former pastor, Antonio Stephenson, used to say, "The only time you should look down on someone is when you are reaching down to pick them up."

Whether we realize it or not, we interpret life through the defective lens of our own eyes and our personal experiences. Once I was older and a bit more experienced with how sour life can be, I was able to give my dad some help.

Brooding on these thoughts made it easier for me to forgive him. All the worries and cares belong to no one else but God. Besides, he was getting older, and I could hear my mother's voice, "No matter what he did or didn't do, he is still your father."

Life throws unending difficulties and challenges at everyone; and, without help, they may spiral downward.

When we see the person who offended us struggling, we should be more ready to forgive.

We should set our emotions aside and say I choose to absolve him no matter what. The rest we can work out daily. The need for forgiveness becomes more apparent when we realize that people lash out when in pain.

Dr. Sandra D. Wilson depicts this situation in her book *Hurt People Hurt People.*

"When we seek to numb the pain of unseen wounds—either knowingly or unknowingly—with denial or other emotional anesthetics, we inevitably create additional pain for us and for others. Rather than acknowledging the existence of our invisible inner injuries and treating them, we often attempt to distance ourselves from them by deflecting our pain onto those around us. And, typically, we hurt others most deeply in the areas of our deepest wounding."

I did not want either my father or myself to follow such an endless cycle of suffering. At the time of these reflections, I was stationed on a ship in Charleston, South Carolina, and planned on soon returning to Texas, where my dad lived.

As I prepared for my journey back to Texas, I anticipated beginning a new relationship with him, though the journey did not come without some hesitation on my part. But then, the word came down from the Captain that we all would be put on a platform to go to the battle zone in Iraq. The thought of going to war and not coming back alive hit me like a ton of bricks.

What would happen to my soul if I died without forgiving my father? The loud thump of my heart started pounding. The thought of spending an eternity in hell brought a hot flash of sweat to my forehead. If I did not remove the iniquity from my heart, reunion with my dad would remain far from me.

- **Understanding the general effect of 'SIN'**

Man was born into sin and will continue until the day he acknowledges God in his life. Once he confesses his numerous sins to God, he's forgiven every one of them. Once we understand our shortcomings before God are just as great as those who offended us, why not forgive? I always say, "I'm not perfect, but I'm a work in progress."

Ephesians 4:32 ESV "Be kind to one another, tenderhearted, forgiving one another, as God in Christ forgave you."

Speak your hurt and pain. Uncover the covered. If

God has forgiven our sins, why then should we not forgive others? To what purpose is our unforgiveness? And yes, how do we say, "Father, forgive me of my sins," if we ourselves cannot forgive another? The Psalmist writes, "If I had cherished sin in my heart, the Lord would not have listened." Ps. 66:18 (NIV) I want God to hear me when I pray. What about you?

CHAPTER 4
Forgiveness And Humility

There was one question I asked myself some time ago, which helped set me on track. However, before I reveal what the question is, let us talk a bit about humility. What does it mean to be humble? Regarding forgiveness, humility is the ability to reflect, express, or offer submission when needed. We will decongest what these terms mean.

Anyone who desires to be humble must be able to reflect on one's actions, both past and present. Peering back at my own life, I bear many faults. My paths were ridden with potholes, so there was not any reason for me to go about with shoulder pads. A proud person sees himself or herself as possessing something others do not have.

Now, here are some of the questions I have asked myself. What exactly did I have that my father didn't have? Was I any better than him? No, I am a work in progress, remember? I had many flaws and areas where I had not done too well. Connecting the two, I had expected too much from my father.

As a kid, you have a hundred and one expectations. When you talk with your friends, they tell you how their fathers take them to parks during the weekend, attend their sporting events, how he read bedtime stories to them at night, and all of those other stories that would leave me wishing for more. I had an "aha" moment. I framed all the things I heard and created a very long list I expected my father to fulfill.

I envisioned him buying me candies, reading stories, dropping me off at school, sitting in the sporting stands watching me play, and more. So, the moment he failed to attend to one of the needs on my list, I would tag him as imperfect. He wasn't there to teach me things only a father could teach his daughter.

He wasn't there to protect me! So, if anyone had asked me then, I would have said he was a lousy father, absentee to the max. However, I failed to consider that I too was not perfect. I am not perfect. I am not the best woman, wife, friend, parent, or saint! I have as many faults as any human being.

Why, then, did I find it hard to forgive him? It was then I began to learn how to be humble. It means a lot that, despite all my faults, God is still very willing to accept me for who I am. He is ready to open his hands to me and forgive me for every one of my sins. I dealt so much with anger, resentment, bitterness, and yes, even hate! Yet, God still welcomed me, promising to help me get better.

From the definition of humility I gave above, we can also see that humility involves the ability to express that one isn't perfect. Now it is revealed I, too, am not perfect. I must show it in my actions and expressions—there, forgiveness buds like a flower.

One beautiful thing is people tend to soften quickly when you familiarize yourself with their pain. Telling a wounded person you've gone through the same pain as him or her is sure to break down the stone wall. I believe my father would breathe free-er and feel lighter if I explained to him that no human being could attain a hundred percent perfection in anything.

Submission is another term tied to humility. Submitting to God means you stop trying to prove yourself right. You stop telling yourself that your inability to forgive is okay. Instead, yield to him by telling him you were wrong. I know this is a tough pill to swallow. It is in this submission you will be able to have the heart to forgive. Until you realize you are wrong, your heart may remain as frigid and set as concrete.

Consider a few points that should push us to be humble:

- **We are creations of God**

Pride and humility cannot coexist. Humility is a term that calls for total dependence on the person of God. It involves us seeing that we are wounded creatures trapped in an animal trap and slowly dying without God. Who can live life in such a trap?

It is permissible to have faith in yourself, but unhealthy confidence in yourself (grandeur), and pride, is seen before the destruction. As a result, you place yourself on a high pedestal no one can reach. It makes you question why you should forgive, and your heart desires punishment for your assailant.

My father knew the Lord but had backslidden. I do not pardon what he did to our family, but my understanding has been enlightened. After all, there was no way he could stop himself from doing the things he did without God's help. There would also not have been a way for me to learn how to conquer bitterness, anger, and malice if God hadn't helped me.

The Bible declares to us that God resists whoever is proud. If you are humble, he gives you grace. Anyone seeking to abide in God's presence must exercise humility despite the urge to cultivate their pain.

God, the highest of all, opened the portals of heaven and came down to earth as a man. Yet, he did not hesitate to take on the form of one lower than Himself.

Through this high degree of humility from him, we became free.

You might consider humility one of the many features that God expects us to bear, however painful it may be. Humility takes the very core of the Christian life. Humility is what draws God closer to his creation.

Humility opens a man's life to the touch and workings of God. Therefore, for everyone and anyone that seeks to pursue the holy things of God, he or she must ensure that humility stands in the same line as love and forgiveness.

It was only later in my Christian race that I realized I had been claiming to be a true disciple of God without being lowly at heart. Fortunately, God helped me to realize this truth and helped me to realize how to chase after being holy. Unlike what most of us think, we do not become humble on our own accord. Humility is achieved by prayer and faith. We can also achieve it by allowing Christ to complete his work in us.

- **The Humility of Jesus**

God depicted times in the Bible when Jesus Christ's humility was brought to the limelight. As Jesus spoke, he always exalted the father. Never for once did he take the glory to himself. Instead, he always spoke of how he was only serving the Father.

Jesus used words like:

- I am come not to do my own will but to do the will of Him that sent me (John 6:38)
- I do nothing of myself, but He who sent me is true (John 7:28)
- These words which you hear are not my own, they belong to the father who sent me (John 14:24)

The humility of Jesus made the redemption he had to offer us effective. We also see that unless God fills us; we will remain as empty vessels. Humility may be one of the hardest goals to achieve, but we can learn from Jesus. Through him, we know this truth—that humility stems from knowing that God works in all to establish that we can do nothing by ourselves. We must constantly depend on God for help in all areas of our lives.

The life Christ wants us to live is one that is dead to both sin and self. He wants us to know that his presence in our lives helps us to be lowly and meek. One thing to note about Jesus is that he wasn't just humble regarding things relating to God. Amidst men, he also remained humble, fetching him a truckload of honor among them. He saw himself as a servant of men, consequently allowing God to work his way to men through him.

If we are to bring these attributes of Jesus into our topic, we will see that the Spirit of forgiveness can only be embedded into us by God. He wants us to realize this very purpose. He would have wanted me to stop struggling to attain perfection early enough. He was probably saying this—daughter, let me get rid of these chains for you.

Jesus never tried to take the glory of all the great work he manifested on earth. His whole life was a total surrender to God. And this example is what every believer out there should follow. Beloved, I have come to ask myself many questions I believe you should ask yourself too.

Are you humble?

The answer to this question lies in your daily routines. Ask your family, ask your friends, ask Jesus. If these entities do not see traces of surrender or lowliness in our lives, we must again learn from Jesus. We have to consider that through his humility, he was able to win so much to himself. The several manifestations of the father through him were only possible because of his humble Spirit.

- **Humility in the teaching of Jesus**

The next thing that can teach us the principles of humility is the teaching of Jesus. Jesus made it known to us how much he expects us to be as humble as he was. The Beatitudes in the Gospel of Matthew direct that the meek shall inherit the earth. He also said that only the poor in Spirit shall have to themselves the Kingdom of heaven. These passages communicate that heaven and earth belong to those who can be lowly in heart.

Another area where he mentioned humility was when his disciples argued about who would be the greatest in the Kingdom. When they asked Jesus, the response he gave them was that the one who humbles himself as a little child would be exalted. Even in heaven, humility takes the rule of the day. Jesus said that the least of the believers would be marked as great.

One perfect display of humility can be seen in John 13:1-5, where Jesus tied a towel around his waist, washed his disciples' feet, then took the towel from around his waist and dried the disciples' feet. (It must be God to lead me to wash someone else's feet. Just saying!) Now, you would agree that he was their Master and the son of God. Yet, he saw no harm in kneeling, cleaning his disciples' feet. If Jesus could demonstrate humility to this great extent, we, as his disciples, should work towards being humble.

I have noticed how little humility is practiced today. Everyone wants to be on a higher cadre than the other. No one is willing to see themselves as equal to another race, or gender, or with the same quality of freedom. Yet, humility guarantees much more than we can ever think possible. It can champion forgiveness, love, quiet strength, and everything that speaks of God.

"Whoever will be chief among you, let him be your servant." What did Jesus mean by saying this? First, consider who a faithful servant is. He is someone that is devoted to the interests, thoughts, and cares of the Master. He also is concerned about what makes his Master truly happy. Do you know that having a spirit that forgives easily is one thing that can make God happy with us? Jesus also bids us to be servants of one another, helping one another build higher levels in Christ.

If we desire a higher life, the key is to go down! Let us seek not to be exalted. We must understand that exaltation comes from God. Therefore, let our principal purpose and prayer be that we humble ourselves. A lowly spirit gravitates to the glory and power of God.

- **Humility in our daily life**

Do you love the Lord genuinely? Do you know that our love for him is weighed through our relationships with Him and man? His Word urges us to let our good works show before men so they may glorify our father in heaven. What kind of attitudes are we displaying before men? Are they acts that cause man to glorify God? Does the lack of a forgiving spirit glorify God?

Paul made it known in his teachings that we should always prefer one another in honor. He also said that we should never set our minds on high things but on lowly things. We should never be wise in our own conceit. This particular statement applies so much to me, you know? I saw my inability to forgive my father as normal. I saw myself as wise, so I found it hard to get to a balanced point.

According to the book of Corinthians, love does not puff itself up or seek its own. Love is not easily provoked! Now, I ask myself this question. If I truly loved my father with God's kind of love, would I have been provoked by the deeds of my father? Would I not have sought ways to let him know of God's mercy and grace? Would I have only thought of myself alone? In hindsight, clearly, he was going through a lot of pain to have been drinking. What was my little way of reaching out to him?

Paul taught another heavy piece of truth. "...bearing graciously with one another, and willingly forgiving each other...just as the Lord has forgiven you, so should you forgive". (Colossians 3:13 AMP) It means that we may be so angry that we may find it acutely hard to forgive. He appeals to us to restrict ourselves from unforgiveness when this happens, knowing God forgave us of our sins.

When we put on the Lord Jesus, we put on compassion, kindness, humility, meekness, and long-suffering. These attributes reveal our Christ-likeness.

• Humility and Holiness

It would have been much easier to assume I was better since I wasn't drinking. I was not the one that abandoned my family. I wasn't the one that ran away from my kids. I was different. I was pure, right? However, I forgot that I also had areas where I lack perfection. The standard for Christian holiness is the holiness of God. That kind of complete holiness can only be achieved with the aid of the Spirit.

Anyone who seeks to be holy must take care so that pride doesn't creep in at some point. The story of the Pharisee and the publican going to the temple to pray is an example in Luke 18:10-14. When pride struck the Pharisee as he worshipped God, he exalted himself by speaking of how good he was. But, on the other hand, the publican could be reckoned by God because of his humility.

My friend, let us never say that we are holier than anyone. The only person who can take such a claim is Christ, who happens to be the humblest of all. What God defines as humility is an inability of him to see *'self'* in a man's life. I wish we could realize that our thoughts, words, and feelings as humans are tools that God uses to test our humility towards him.

No pride can be as dangerous as the pride that comes from an unhealthy sense of self-empowerment. When this pride creeps into people, it takes settlement in how they converse, act, and carry themselves. So, Friends, we should beware! That way, we will not live in false humility only to discover that God never did reckon with us at the end of the day.

- **Humility and Sin**

The best scripture to help us understand the relationship between humility and sin is written in the first book of Timothy 1:15. There, we see this scriptural verse —*'Sinners, of whom I am chief.'* How could someone who had done so much for God call himself a sinner? Most people would refer to this as the utterance of false words. However, his words only express how humble he was.

Paul constantly referred to himself as the least and how he felt unworthy of being called an apostle. The lesson we should draw from his words is that the secret to humility is buried in us, always realizing that we are sinners saved by God's grace.

Before Paul had a relationship with the Lord, he had sinned terribly by persecuting the church. So, every time, he took joy in confessing how the grace and mercy of God had been made available to him, the worst of sinners.

Paul's words also help us realize that the only reason he could stop doing the wrong things he did in the past was that God restricted him. God is a being that will always prevent us from sinning against him if we choose to yield. In the book of Romans, Paul also talked about there being no good thing in his flesh. Therefore, this flesh is naturally prone to doing the wrong things.

Man's lack of a forgiving spirit proves that our hearts, mind, and souls need light. It means that we need healing from God. We need good health from God, as only this health can swallow up the disease eating away at us. His light kills the darkness within us, and we rise as great expellers of light. This process manifests as us being under the mercy and love of God.

One mistake several people make today is by thinking that humility concerning sin means condemning one's self. On the contrary, what makes us humble is the revelation of the grace and mercy of God shed abroad in our hearts.

We take glory in the fact that God delivered us from the past's chains and struggles. A sinner who dwells in the full light of God's love and has experienced the joy that comes from dwelling in the presence of God cannot help but live humbly.

- **Humility and Faith**

Many of us know of the joy, peace, and healing that God's presence brings to us. We have seen it, read about it, and even received teachings about it. However, no matter how much we try to key into these possibilities, it seems like there is a hindrance somewhere. What could be the cause of this? Can we call it the lack of faith?

Faith, humility, and love are features that a Christian must have as the very roots of his life. Let us start this section by understanding what faith is. It is a situation where we confess our helplessness to God and how much we are willing to allow God to work in our lives. Faith also means that we key into the beautiful things and miracles that he has wrought in the life of other Christians.

Faith is the exact tool through which we tap into the world of blessings God offers his children. Faith helps us seek after a touch that comes only from God and even believe that God truly exists.

Bitterness and anger might be words that people speak of; however, when those emotions develop roots in the heart, it could be like pulling wisdom teeth to uproot them. Faith allows us to believe right in the healing abilities of God. The only thing that makes it impossible to have this faith is pride. In other words, faith, humility, and love coexist.

Love and humility make our hearts ready to trust in God. The one way we honor God is by trusting totally in him. Jesus also pointed out the tie between humility and faith when he marveled at the centurion's faith. The man told Jesus he was not worthy to have him under his roof. His great humility helped him get rid of everything that stood as a barrier to faith.

Have we not done wrong by the struggle to believe in God? And yet, we have sought to take hold of the blessing and riches he pours upon our lives. The first way out of this issue is to change our ways. Earnestly pray for the humility that comes from God. Let our love for God overshadow our pride in life. It is through this humility our hearts can be purged.

Nothing will eliminate the pain and anger that comes when men refuse to give us the recognition we deserve to receive. But I've learned the one distinction we should seek is the one that comes from God. The glory of men and self comes and goes with the wave of time. So, the stronger we grow in our faith, the more we will be able to present ourselves humbly before him.

I would love to relate my personal experience to the relationship between humility, faith, and forgiveness. I was already at the point where my heart had become saturated with too many wrong thoughts, and I was struggling big time. I struggled to forgive and bring my life to the point of balance. But I found God at work in my life when nothing else worked.

What a beautiful thing he helped me to realize that the secret to winning is the Spirit he places in us. He put something 'extra' in me that fought powerfully against my struggles. This extra thing comprises faith, humility, love, and the Spirit of forgiveness.

CHAPTER 5
Faith and Forgiveness

In the previous chapter, we discussed the touch forgiveness has on faith. However, the touch faith has on forgiveness is paramount. You must come to a point where you have faith in God and not yourself. How can we achieve this?

Consider when someone has a very severe headache. A couple of pills down the throat, and the pain is less severe, yes? Now, such an act is known as the pain-medication bond. This same effect also applies to the ointment you rub against your skin when you have a sprain or muscle ache.

When considering the inability to forgive, I devised it to encompass untouched pain. For me, it started with unmet expectations and then the torment of heartbreak. If you have ever suffered heartbreak, you may relate. For those who have not suffered a heartbreak, here is some relatable information you can oblige.

The anguish does not come from the muscles of the heart or chest. It is a woe that arises from dashed hopes and a million other rationalizations. You think of how much you loved them and expected much from them. You think of how much they disappointed and hurt you, and the hurt that stirs up from it feels so strong you can hardly breathe.

Following the agony of heartbreak came the pain of abandonment. When my father avoided my sister and me even after we searched for him, I felt great lamentation in my heart. Then, I found myself asking numerous unhealthy questions:

Were we not wanted? Were we a burden to him? Did he hate us so much that he would dart off into the woods on that dark night? Were our efforts to search for him not appreciated? Had he cut us off forever? Did we hurt him?

As the train of thoughts hibernates within the mind of anyone without any particular answer, such a person could suffer low self-esteem. This condition is defined by one feeling less of oneself. You begin to wonder if you weren't enough for the person.

You wonder if someone ever found joy just by staying with you and exchanging stories. You do wonder if that person ever loved you. Usually, the only answers one gets from these questions are those that push the heart deep into the wells of anguish.

Of course, if my father loved me, he would not have left. So, I concluded he didn't love me. This conclusion bred anger, hatred, and malice in my heart. I hated to hear anyone talk about him. I hated to think of him. When I saw other kids with their fathers, I presumed the love wasn't real. This bitterness that grew in my heart ate deeply into me and birthed the subsequent pain—the pain of frustration.

You see everyone next to you wearing big smiles. You see everyone looking free and excited about their new turns. Looking in the mirror at your life, it seems you have never moved from the point you have always occupied. It appears your life has only presented itself to struggle. Then, you begin to get angry and tired of chasing your potential. You see everything as a waste. You feel nothing deserves your attention or time.

Don't normalize the struggle.

At this point, I cannot help but sigh deeply. What possible medication could bring healing to such a hurt individual? Honestly, if someone had offered me a pill that could have helped me forget all the pain and horrible experiences, I'd have swallowed it down my throat without entertaining a single questioning thought.

What if my father went through this exact same predicament? Maybe there was something he combatted and desperately desired liberation. Unfortunately, the only pill that could have worked in masking that pain for him was alcohol. At this stage, people try out a whole bulk of things that they think will help take away the searing pain.

These measures lay a lot of deceitfulness since it would appear as if they were working as medications. After all, they only mask the actual effect of pain for a while. Yes, the pain is still significant, alive, and growing. My father probably realized this fact and then decided to spend most of his life under the influence of alcohol.

There is one medication that completely erases the pain of the past. It is not pleasure, money, alcohol, fame, or other deceitful pills. It is forgiveness. Forgiveness is a simple word that works out more wonders than any other thing.

You would ask me, how can I forgive? I would ask you, why not forgive? You might also say, O', and it is not easy to forgive. Shaking my head in agreement, I respond that I know all too well. That is why I am going to expose to you another secret—Faith. What is that? Is it a pill? No, it is not. Faith is a medication that deals with the root cause of the pain you feel. The root cause is known as the lack of a forgiving spirit.

For someone who does not know the Lord, how can you achieve this faith? Faith comes by hearing, Apostle Paul said, and hearing by the word of God. The word of God gives you the *'faith'* necessary for salvation, the faith necessary to forgive. Will anyone believe in the Lord without first hearing the word of God? The key to someone suddenly believing in the supernatural is buried right in the word.

You might have heard of how the power of God healed people with severe conditions, yes? The lame walked. The sick with incurable diseases were healed completely. What do you think activated the healing in them? Faith, of course! For example, when Paul wanted to heal the crippled man at Lystra, he preached the gospel first. You read the seventh verse of the fourteenth chapter of Acts. After the man heard the word of God, faith stirred within him. It was that faith that had him jumping to his feet shortly after.

So, it should not matter if you have never been to church in years. Neither does it matter if you have doubts about the supernatural. Seek a reliable source that speaks the true word of God. The word has the natural ability to stir up faith in anyone. The Word of God is powerful and pierces deeply into the dividing asunder of soul and spirit.

From the book of Romans, Paul teaches, "For I am not ashamed of the gospel of Christ: for it is the power of God unto salvation to every one that believeth; to the Jew first, and also to the Greek." 1:16 (KJV) The word of God is what saves any man! It is the power of God unto deliverance, healing, and moving beyond our minute imaginations. It is God's power to free from anger, pain, and most importantly, the lack of a forgiving spirit.

Hebrews chapter eleven and verse one captured my heart many years ago. It talks about the "Now faith" and faith being the substance to things hoped for. People see the word 'Now' and think it is a conjunction, binding the words together. I see it as a command of action—now faith, faith in the present moment. I shared a personal story I titled "Battleground Faith" that I wrote for *Our Story Magazine*. Here is the part I'd like to share with you:

"What joy that filled my soul. Not just to be back in Texas, but before the transfer, I found out I was pregnant with my second child. My first pregnancy was early in my Navy career while I was stationed on a ship in Charleston, South Carolina. That pregnancy ended in a miscarriage. My husband and I were devastated. So, you see why carrying this baby to full term was so important.

I began cramping one evening. The pain was so bad my husband took me to the DFW hospital emergency room. The doctors did a pelvic exam and lab work and concluded I needed an ultrasound to determine if I was having another miscarriage. God and I started having the conversation again of Psalm 34:7 ...Delight and desire. Delight and desire. I whispered the words in my heart. Delight **is** defined in Oxford as taking "great pleasure." "To delight yourself in the Lord is to desire and enjoy the nearness of His presence and the truth and righteousness of His Word." (Life in the Spirit Study Bible) I heard the ultrasound technician say, "I can't see or hear a heartbeat. I'm sorry ma'am."

The war was on. I felt the technician was listening as I talked to God. The WORD is a surefire weapon against the enemy. I believe what the word of God says. Every scripture I could think of at that moment, I uttered.

I exhaled, "I desire to delight in you, Father." By this time, a man in blue scrubs said, "I'm ready to take her." ER staff had already contacted the Operating room and informed them of the presumed miscarriage and the warrant for surgery. I peered at the technician. Turning my head, I gazed beyond the ceiling and into the night sky, and my heart called on the Lord.

The technician ordered the man to stand by for one last scan. She put the doppler on my abdomen, and we waited.... there it was, my baby's heartbeat. She turned the screen for me to see. I saw this grain size of a heartbeat going up and down on the black and gray screen. She yelled back at the man, "I see the heartbeat. I see the heartbeat. We don't need you. Thank you". The man left, and the technician stared at me and said, "Wow, that was something. How did that happen?" I replied, "That was God."

Six months into the pregnancy, the melody from the song "It Takes Faith" released by the Williams Brothers in 1986 danced in my ears. I stepped out in faith to what the doctors and ER staff thought was no heartbeat. Yet, I believed there was something there. When our baby girl was born, we named her Faith, and every time I see her, I am reminded to "Have faith in God" **Mark 11:22.**

It is my hope and prayer that you stand on your faith in the battleground of life. Yes, that little grain that's locked inside of you. When you act on your faith you will find that God is faithful. **(1 Cor 1:9)** There is hope for your hopelessness. There is joy and laughter for your sadness. There is peace for your storm. There is victory in your battles. **It just takes a little faith!**"[1]

Faith in God is very synonymous with confidence in his word. So, when you hear a comment about how the Lord is the strength of your life, you can believe it is right. You read the scripture and see a verse that says *the Lord is my shepherd, I shall not want.* You hear a word of how the stripes of Jesus make you healed, and you key right into it. These words are passageways that lead to spiritual realities and possibilities in the word of God doing virtually the impossible!

Your faith is what causes your hopes to become material. Hope intermingles with faith. It cannot do the mirage alone. It is merged heavily with faith, like a complete trust (with zero doubt) that your hopes would be brought to fulfillment. A man with hope believes that he will have his healing. A man with faith says he will have his healing now, and he is earnest about it.

The words of Jesus are relevant here in Mark 11:23 KJV,

> *"For verily I say unto you, That whosoever shall say unto this mountain, Be thou removed, and be thou cast into the sea;*

> *and shall not doubt in his heart, but shall believe that those things which he saith shall come to pass; he shall have whatsoever he saith."*

How do I know I have the faith that resonates with God? How am I sure I am not just hoping that this will happen? It doesn't seem very clear. Here is how to know. Someone who hopes, agrees that the word of God is capable of causing the changes he needs.

In doubt, for some reason, he feels he will not be able to get it. On the other hand, someone with genuine faith in God believes that as long as God has spoken it, then so be it. Even though it is not tangible yet, I believe and have faith that I have it.

Faith is the evidence of the things not seen. Again, the first step to take is to believe God's words. Jesus spoke about this in Mark 11:24—what things soever you desire, when ye pray, BELIEVE that you receive them, and ye shall HAVE them. Indeed, the key to receiving something is first to believe. Believe in the word of God. Believe in his promises.

Believing in God may be scary for some. The uncertainty of his existence or that he will come through for you makes you doubt yourself before you start. You probably have never had any encounter with the Lord and are trying so hard to believe what his word is saying.

It is no secret that the option to overcome resides in your relationship with Him.

Read and study his word. Try him, see if anything the Lord ever said turned out to be a lie. See if he turned out to be incapable of doing what he promised. The Bible assures us that God is not a man who will lie; neither is he the son of man who will repent. Everything he says he will do, he will do, with no alterations later. He is the One you can put your trust in!

Our faith should also not be in what we see or the circumstances around us. I believe I can be free from my struggles because the word of God says it. I believe in my healing because the word of God says it. I don't think it is because I've seen others talk about how God's words freed them. Through these very thoughts, our faith renders us the necessary results.

So many people pray and do not get results because they have not come to the point where they see themselves with the answer. The only thing their eyes get drawn to is how everything seems to get worse. The happenings around us march us more in the paths of unbelief. What unbelief does is cancel the effects of the prayers we have made to God.

Dear one, never base your faith on the happenings around you or on what your mind tells you. Instead, base your faith on the word of God. God, who is not a liar, declares—"I will never leave thee, nor forsake (abandon, leave high and dry, leave stranded) thee. So that we may boldly say, The Lord is my helper, and I will not fear what man shall do unto me." (Heb 13:5b-6 KJV emphasis added).

My friend, no matter how deeply man may hurt you, repeat after me, "The Lord is my helper." Come on, say it again. "The Lord is my helper." Now walk in that! He is THE ONE that will help you to forgive. He is THE ONE that will help you take off the garment of anger, malice, and hatred.

The story takes another turn for those who already feel forsaken by the Lord. Most people believe they are struggling and having hard times in their lives because God left them. I will repeat this fact: God will never leave or forsake you! Faithful is the God that has given unto us this very promise. Instead of uttering words that minister zero healing to you, use words like these—"The Lord is my helper."

When you think about how much that person hurt you, confess this again—"The Lord is my helper." I shall not fear what man shall do unto me.

You cannot help but shed a few tears when you see yourself struggling so hard. Confess this again and again —"The Lord is my helper!"

The more you say it, your belief lathers more and more; and, at that moment, you begin to see things from a different perspective. Never give up on yourself! Never give up on your healing! And never, ever give up on God. He has not given up on you!

THE HEART OF MAN

A man's heart is one of the crucial points to discuss in the relationship between faith and forgiveness. Faith forms in the heart of man. It is also the place where doubt can arise. You might have wondered what it means to believe with one's heart. How does a man believe in a muscular organ that pumps blood to other body parts? Is that even possible?

Yes, it's possible! The physical heart will never be able to birth something as powerful as faith. We are referring to something more substantial and more inclined to the spiritual. This heart is the very center of a man known as the Spirit of man. If we desire God or want to obtain anything he offers, we must use the tools that echo him.

For example, if you have ever worked with screws and screwdrivers, you will realize that the mouth of a screwdriver must fit in with the head of the screw for there to be any observable movement or turn. If we apply this same principle, we discover that those who connect with God—a spirit—must do so in the 'spirit' form. The Bible says that God is a Spirit, and they that worship him must worship him in spirit and truth. (John 4:24)

Our body or mind will never be able to connect to God on that level. Only our spirit can do that. Understanding that you are a spirit living within a body is crucial at this point. The spirit of man is the bearer of a man's soul, and it is this soul's responsibility to make the emotional, intellectual, and spiritual calculations. When you were born again, the metamorphosis of your spirit man was taking place.

Being born-again is a spiritual adventure where God begins to bring his light to you. The area of contact between you and God is your spirit, which is also your heart. The first book of Corinthians 2:14 holds the truth of the matter—"But the natural man receiveth not the things of the Spirit of God: for they are foolishness unto him: neither can he know them, because they are spiritually discerned." (KJV)

The Word of God is of God's spirit, and the mind will never be able to understand it. It is the spirit man that helps to make a useful connection with the word of God. That is why allowing the Holy Spirit to reveal the depth of God's word to us is necessary. When we talk about believing the word of God with our hearts, we talk about accepting the word of God with our spirit.

Consider the words of Solomon in Proverbs 3:5-7a— "Trust in the LORD with all thine heart; And lean not unto thine own understanding. In all thy ways acknowledge him, And he shall direct thy paths. Be not wise in thine own eyes:" (KJV) What this scripture is essentially trying to tell us is that the directions our human mind gives us will continually fail us. They only lead us to paths that satisfy the flesh, which is totally against what God has for us.

I researched ways to train my heart to carry the right things. I Googled, read books and magazines, and watched clips on YouTube. I started comparing notes from the reference and found a lot of helpful information. I then took my journal and began to write my list of bullet points. I exhaled in awe when I finished.

- **Meditate on the word of God**

Meditation is one way to harness the value of God's word. Meditation unlocks the hidden potential in God's word and makes it realistic. We open our hearts and minds, and transformation occurs from the inside out.

God revealed to Joshua the power of meditation—"This book of the law shall not depart out of thy mouth; but thou shalt meditate therein day and night, that thou mayest observe to do according to all that is written therein: for then thou shall make thy way prosperous, and then thou shall have good success." Joshua 1:8 KJV

You must craft in time for meditation. How, one may ask, amidst the business of family, work, and extracurricular activities with the kids? First, go to a quiet place where you know you will not be disturbed by noise or other distractions. The human mind is one of the sources of the noises spoken of here.

You want to ensure you can push your Spirit into a calm place. You must not focus on all your worries, fears, and cares in these moments. Deep breath in, then exhale. Allow yourself to fill your imagination with the word of God. Then, allow the Spirit of God to speak to you. And most importantly, LISTEN!

- **Live out the word of God.**

Living out the word of God involves carrying out every instruction in the ability God has rendered to me. For example, one of the instructions that correlates to the topic of forgiveness is this: "A new commandment I give unto you, love one another; as I have loved you, so you must love one another." John 13:34 NIV

This scripture says the reason we should love someone should be more because Christ also loves us. Someone who lives by the word will follow this very commandment. Will it come easily? At times yes; other times, there will be challenges.

One more truth is found in Philippians 4:7 KJV—"And the peace of God, which passeth all understanding, shall keep your hearts and minds through Christ Jesus." Just as a blanket can make your body feel warm on a cold day, the Holy Spirit can give your spirit a feeling of warmth and peace. This passage is saying to you and me to let God do it. Let God keep the peace in our hearts and our minds. We, of limited power, cannot do this. Only God can. However, living out God's word is the key to accessing this peace.

- **Give the word of God first place**

I will be the first to say I am guilty of putting other things before God. Would you be the second to say this? Hey, it's okay; we're all in the boat together. We must make every effort to put our priorities in order—God is first place in our hearts.

God's position in place matters so much during your healing time. In Proverbs 4, we see God urging us to constantly attend to his words and gravitate our ears to his sayings. He inclines us further not to let his words depart from our eyes. They should be kept right in our hearts.

God's urge is because he knows the amount of change and healing that his word can do in our life if we continue to put him first. He knows about the pressures that push you to the limit. So, every time you feel overwhelmed in your spirit, hurry to give God's word prevalence.

- **Listen to the voice of the Lord**

> *The* L*ORD* *said, "Go out and stand on the mountain in the presence of the* L*ORD**, for the* L*ORD* *is about to pass by." Then a great and powerful wind tore the mountains apart and shattered the rocks before the* L*ORD**, but* **the** L**ORD** **was not in the wind.** *After the wind, there was an earthquake, but* **the** L**ORD** **was not in the earthquake.** *After the earthquake came a fire, but* **the** L**ORD** **was not in the fire.** *And after the fire came a gentle whisper. When Elijah heard it, he pulled his cloak over his face and went out and stood at the mouth of the cave. 1 Kings 19:11-13 (NIV)*

Here the Lord is giving Elijah a revelation, but not in the manner we may think. It wasn't loud and forthcoming to startle you. It came in the voice of a gentle whisper. Yes, the spirit has a voice, just like how you have a mouth that utters words. For this very purpose, building up your spirit with the word of God is essential. You know what comes from God and what does not. The word of God enriches your heart so that what it speaks to you is what God would want you to do.

There are a lot of voices out there. Many sound like the right voice. We put the words of these voices into practice only to conclude that it was not the right voice after all. Doubling back on my experience, I listened to those negative voices concerning my dad, my self-esteem, and my value.

The grudge I bore towards my father was as big as Texas. But the negative self-talk was more dangerous. I believed the first fueled the second. As a result, I began to harbor depraved thoughts and unsavory words against him. Honestly, if you heard me utter these words, you may doubt my Christianity for a second.

I know there are many people just like me struggling to kill the part of them that voices out strongly to those they have come to hate. They have tried to stop it, but reflecting on the acts displayed to them by the offender makes it hard to shake loose. The only secret I can reveal here is the secret of training.

For instance, when a child eats foods mostly rich in carbohydrates, you may find the child grows out with skinny arms and a slightly bulging belly. This same concept can be applied to our lives. The more we feed our spirit with hatred and anger, the more wrong words we utter. God discourages this and encourages us to provide our hearts with his word. After this happens, your heart will be able to offer you the necessary medications when the onset of the sharp prick of anger begins. He's waiting for us to tap into what he has provided.

You cannot do it alone!

This truth is something my grandmother would always tell me. "You take one step; God will take two." She meant we also have parts to play in the healing process. God does more of the work, of course. But, first, you must trust God to start and finish the process. I will say it again, your faith is what accelerates the promises of God. Your faith is what makes the promises of God's healing substantial.

In the next chapter, we will delve into the process of forgiveness. I was ready for the finished product without going through the process. That is not how it works. We cannot learn what we need to know by skipping to the end. We learn as we go through the process. So, keep reading, and let us grow together!

---

1. Williams, Cassie J. *"Battleground Faith"*. Article. Our Story Magazine: Hope & Inspiration for Seasons of Life & Grace. Winter Issue 2021. pg 91-93

CHAPTER 6
Forgiveness' Opened Door

In a 2008 article from the Open to Hope Foundation, Dr. Frederic Luskin, Ph.D., writes,

---

"The process of forgiveness can be a liberating experience, one that, if practiced proactively, can lead to a wonderful quality of life. Interestingly, forgiveness can only occur because we have been given the gift of choice. We have the *choice* to forgive or not to forgive, and no one can force us to do either. Conversely, if we want to forgive someone, no one can stop us. This ability to forgive is a manifestation of the personal control we have over our lives."

"If we want to forgive someone, no one can stop us."

In the first chapter, I spoke of how forgiveness has depth, length, and width. It's a three-dimensional entity that leads right into a labyrinth. In this labyrinth are different stages, processes, and phases. Skip one of them, and you get lost in the complicated web. In understanding these phases, frustrations may occur, but press on. In this section, I will take you through the once-closed door of forgiveness that I forgave my father and others who had hurt me.

1. **Incorporate the Principle of unconditional love**

Unconditional love is the first Principle to support the melting away of an unsympathetic heart. When the unconditional love of God resonates in your thought process, the rationale is undeniable. To forgive inherits no payback from the offender. **Forgiveness is not for sale; it is given.** So, for us to for-give, we need to give forgiveness.

Why I Stayed: The Choices I Made in My Darkest Hour by Gayle Haggard is a story of and life of unconditional love. Gayle, the wife of megachurch Pastor Ted Haggard, chose to stay with her husband after inappropriate relationships and drug use. She chose to forgive Ted and work through the process of forgiveness amidst the pain, hurt, and disgrace. Unfortunately, being in the public eye made it even more difficult.

I was in my mid-thirties when I saw the news flash on my television screen. Ted had resigned from his position as Lead Pastor of the church in Colorado Springs and was walking down a road working at his new job of delivering supplies. The newscaster was walking beside him, asking him questions. You could see Ted's frustration, but he kept his head forward and feet marching on, trying not to let the media distract or discourage him.

Behind the closed doors, Gayle and Ted sat down, and he willingly told her to ask him any questions. Many talks went on as well as marriage counseling. Gayle felt Ted had Godly sorrow for what he had done. He began to prove his love and commitment to earning back her love and trust. She chose to forgive him. I felt that this book replicates that no sin, confessed, and true-to-the-heart repentance would be able to separate one from God's forgiveness, love, and mercy.

Although I had made many errors, his love remained independent of my wrong acts and ways of living. He alone had the secret to the mystery of 'unconditional love.' So, if I were to live differently, I had to first learn of him.

2. Acknowledge the hurt

I believe the one thing absent from us all is the acknowledgment of the negativity the offense has caused. How deeply did the pain affect you? What parts of your life were restricted? We all want to act like the hurt doesn't damage us, yet we are still wounded!

We all want to make it look like we can live off what they did, but we cannot! We think of it every minute, second, and hour. And you would agree with me that it is this very act that causes the anger in us to grow. We get mad because we cannot live off the blame.

Please think of the person that hurt you and why you think they did what they did. Under what situation did the incident occur? Do you know of anything they had to battle at that time? How long ago did the incident occur? In answering these questions, you may begin to understand the person that hurt you with a little more clarity. In addition, you get to see things from their perspective, which can bring a better understanding.

There are cases where people are too angry even to consider forgiveness. As a choice, people keep it at the back of their minds forever, cultivating their hearts to harden. If you engage in this class, you have my understanding. But bring yourself to the realization that the grudge you have kept in your heart might just be hindering you from a better joy. So, even if it hurts, consider what you can gain with a free heart. And if it gets too hard for you, do not hesitate to talk to someone about it. A trusted friend or counselor is a phone call away.

3. Accept the incident

Realize the person cannot undo what has been done. What you can do is allow space for healing and move on. This acceptance ends unnecessary thoughts and the build-up of anger. Accept that no matter how angry you get, the past can never be undone. But you can be restored. You can be whole again.

I saw no reason to remain angry with my father or others. I had not seen him in years and did not know how he fared. Maybe he replaced his love for my siblings and me with alcohol; who knows? To what purpose, then, would I keep my grudge and remain in a state of suffering?

In 1991, while serving on a ship in Charleston, South Carolina, I received a message stating I would possibly deploy to serve in the Iran/Iraq war. I made all the necessary pre-deployment plans. At peace with my husband and God—check. Bills and finances—check. I spoke to Mom and siblings—check. Reconciliation with my dad—oh NO, not checked.

Determined to fully accept what had happened and eliminate the iniquity in my heart, I resolved to take leave and visit my father. Hopefully, I would find him sober. Hopefully, he won't dart away again. Perhaps we could talk things through. This was my prayer. I was curious to listen to his side of the story. I would choose to forgive him without hesitation. Of course, it may not be as simple as I have summarized it, but I knew I could do this with God.

4. Repair the broken bond

First, I will say that some bonds cannot be repaired. Mending the broken bond between two offenses requires both parties to agree. Despite what preceded, the decision to forgive requires only one yes. That yes could only be yours.

At this stage, I considered how I could help dad out of whatever despair life might have thrown him. I listened to his struggles. I shared with him how much I struggled. Finally, I told him how I could come to terms with forgiving him.

You should note that the relationship may take some time to bounce back to the same level it was before. You may not want it to bounce back to what it was before. Instead, you want it to be better and stronger with more life.

With time comes healing. With patience comes trust. Just ensure that you are deliberate about your actions. If possible, continue to reach out to them. You will make them wonder what suddenly happened to you.

My actions are what God required of me...and you. God wanted me to be free. He also wanted my dad to be free. God wants you to be free! What if God allowed me to go through this because he wanted to teach me a key that would help thousands of people draw near to him? My prayer for you and me is that we never miss God's path for us to thread through.

5. **Lessons learned**

I got to a point where I could look back at what happened and chuckle freely. No painful tears or anger arose. Instead, I received closure for that account. I could not believe I was that person. Perhaps you will see the strong person you have become. Your efforts at achieving forgiveness are worth it at this stage. You wish you would have started earlier.

You should know that it is not every time the person you have a grudge toward will be willing to give you an audience. Sometimes, they may still be as stubborn and annoying as they used to be. Do not bring an end to your journey to forgiveness as a result.

Save the health of your mind and heart by forgiving. You may also pray for the person who wronged you. It's hard to hate someone you are praying for. Ask God to help soften his or her heart. Ask God to forgive them because they may not know what they are doing. Remember, Jesus asked the Father to forgive those who charged him guilty and sentenced him to death. God delights in such acts of his children.

6. Visit a therapist if needed

For those with the following side effects—trauma, nightmares, suicidal thoughts, thoughts of hurting others, etc., I want to encourage you to connect with a counselor or therapist. You could also talk to a friend in the fellowship if you trust the person's decisive abilities.

Sometimes, unforgiveness carries a weight like a ball and chain. It could get life-draining and exhaustive. Combine your therapy sessions with the secret ingredient of prayer and you will be well on your way to a completed meal. Remember, the issues of the heart can only be settled by God. My grandmother's words are relevant right now—you take one step, and God will take two. Now, the door is open, walk through.

CHAPTER 7
Finding a Purpose for Forgiveness

The doctor comes in as I sit in the chair anxiously awaiting my test results. You know how we get when we want everything to be okay, but we prepare for a hiccup. "Your test looks good," she reports, "Your A1C is within normal limits."

I exhale at the news because an elevated A1C would mean I would have diabetes and would have to go on medicine. Diabetes is prevalent in my family and silently etches its way into one's body from an unhealthy lifestyle or family history. "You are doing well, so keep up the good work, eating right and exercising, and I will see you again in six months," she adds.

A week later, I ran on the treadmill after doing my morning stretches. The weather was cold and muggy, so running on the treadmill inside would certainly be better than a runny nose later. Instead of listening to motor-racing music, I decided to YouTube motivational speakers. As my left foot stepped on the treadmill, my index finger tapped a YouTube video.

A laugh from deep within the speaker's stomach met my ears. I stopped in wonder for a moment, but then I began to laugh along, not knowing why I was laughing. Fortunately, I had not hit the start button on the treadmill; otherwise, the laugh might have ended in tears.

My ears were met by an intensely deep voice of confidence I had never heard in that genre. I had heard of Les Brown in passing, but he was mostly unknown to me. He was talking about dreams, life, and people's potential. "Move on, suck it up, get over it," he said, "Take ownership of your life."

I thought about the doctor's results and the encouragement to keep exercising. I was taking ownership of my life and health, not wanting to be sick with diabetes. I wanted to be healthy. But was I allowing unforgiveness to take ownership of me, or was I taking ownership of unforgiveness?

Forgiveness and "your why" are closely interrelated. To know *"Why not forgive?"* you must first find a purpose for forgiveness. In other words, what is your "Why?" Let me explain. The purpose or why is defined as the reason backing up an action or decision. The purpose or why is that very thing that keeps anyone motivated. The purpose or why is a REMINDER of one's plans and goals concerning a particular situation.

Knowing "Why" is a foundation you can always fall back on when things do not go as planned. You could be sailing so smoothly that you think you have got everything right. Then, one day, everything begins to spiral down and you wonder what went wrong. You begin to feel pressed by the same walls you pushed against years ago. Your purpose, your why, is what keeps you from giving up. Your purpose is the adrenaline pump that keeps you motivated.

How do you find your why? How can someone who has been hurt for so long find a purpose in forgiving? What should be considered? Let us look at the choices to work with:

UNDERSTANDING *WHY* FORGIVENESS MATTERS

You might want to tell yourself this a thousand times over—*Forgiveness does matter.* Between that intense feeling of dislike and forgiveness is a line that most people do not see the need to cross. They feel that nothing is going to change by their forgiving; however, a whole lot of things change when forgiveness sets in.

First, did you know that forgiving a person will go a long way in boosting that energy and strength within you? If you forgive another, you suddenly feel empowered and ready to face the world. What changed? Why do you think you would not have felt that way if holding a grudge? The answer is that internal struggles never make anyone happy. The only thing they do is stir up frustration, and that, my friend, can be very draining.

When someone hurts you deeply, you become like a snail. You gather up every fold of yourself and then withdraw into your shell. Why? You want to protect yourself from more hurt. You see everyone with clubs and daggers aimed at your heart. However, in the process, you lose out on developing absolute and solid friendships. You shut yourself out from the joy and abundance life has to give.

In the previous chapter, we discussed how *'learning of lessons'* can be one of the steps that leads to forgiveness. If you fail to learn the lessons, you may expose yourself to the risk of another person hurting you. In addition, if you refuse to assess the situation to learn the areas you need to work on, the risk is that you may suffer more than you ever planned. You may be left wondering if you have control of the issue or if you are worthy of real love, and peace.

You are worthy of every good thing that exists. You are worthy of love, joy, peace, and everything God has planned for you. See yourself stepping into a significant healing phase and developing a purpose. Prolonged anger and the lack of a forgiving spirit can lead to many other issues you want to avoid. Some of them are the following:

- Anxiety
- Depression/low self-esteem/low self-worth
- PTSD symptoms
- Trauma
- Nightmares
- High blood pressure
- Insomnia
- Loneliness
- Bitterness

Not to mention other cancers of the heart. Though the list is endless, these few should scare you away from holding on to that ball and chain, the grudge that makes you live less. I love being able to breathe freely and being healthy. We all like it when people say we are taking care of ourselves and look younger than our actual age. Forgiveness allows us to live life to the fullest. We owe ourselves that, at least.

PREPARING YOURSELF AHEAD REDUCES INJURIES

My husband has been a coach and personal trainer for almost thirty years. I hear stories of athletes wanting to get to the next level but being unwilling to do the hard work necessary. Often, he says he must help someone shift his mindset to his "why" and coach him in that area before the actual physical work can begin. Case in point, if someone has never lifted weights before, you would not expect him to storm into a gym and instantly become a professional bodybuilder. No personal trainer should give anyone that false hope.

Muscles might get strained, bones fractured, and self-esteem shattered. There is a process that must take place. You would instruct a beginner to start with the lighter weights and slowly move on to the heavier ones. You would notice how his muscles slowly adjusted as the load impacted on them. Body builders begin with the light weights, and repetitions and sets. Over time, they are ready for a heavier load.

Unforgiveness is a weight. A heavy one at that. You may start forgiving the minor offenses other people offer you. That someone hurts you deeply, one time, does not mean that he or someone else will not hurt you again.

More people might say more hurtful things to you. More people might do something worthy of your keeping grudges. But you should not wait for that to happen. If one grudge proved hard to get rid of, you can only imagine how two or more would feel.

Whenever someone hurts you, forgive them. Tell yourself you are not ready to delve deeply into another well of struggles and frustration. Look over any insult thrown your way. Close your eyes to harmful interactions, then focus on building yourself. You will find it easier to tackle the big issue if you have always dealt with it little by little.

This principle is what ants use. When ants come across something too big to be moved at once, they chop it off in small bits and pieces and transport it. Before they have even realized it, most of the obstacles will have been removed. So, train yourself to forgive minor incidents. Allow yourself to believe that not everyone is the same. Please open your eyes to the treasure locked in the people you know by tagging each of them as unique.

You can train yourself by showing love to people. Wear a smile when you walk, talk, and work. Take out time to listen to people talk about their issues. Chuckle freely when someone mistakenly steps on your newly-polished shoes. Yes, I know, that can be very annoying. However, you should do that for yourself. When someone snaps at you, do not be in a hurry to talk back at them.

Think before you speak. Words can tear down or build up. Choose to build up. Situations in which you imagine yourself as being in higher cadres than those who hurt you may also make it hard for you to show this love. Forgiveness is impossible when pride settles in a person. The key to establishing harmony is to focus on your purpose—releasing unforgiveness. Forgive others just as God forgives you of your sins. Always seek out ways to inspire yourself. Read books, attend seminars, and ask questions.

FORGIVING YOURSELF

Maybe you are frowning as you read the title of this section. Is it possible to have something to forgive about oneself? If that is what you are thinking, stay with me. Do you recognize that there have been many times when you were intentionally strict with yourself? I am the same.

Do you realize that you have difficulty loving yourself purposefully? Have you sometimes thought of all the wrong steps you've taken, due to holding a grudge, and have you hated yourself for feeling this way?

Now, here is one thing you need to know. Forgiving others will help you forgive yourself. Self-love allows you to feel a greater sense of self-worth and self-esteem. Open ways through which you can learn to honor yourself. Do not allow a feeling of guilt to result in you trying to give yourself punishments or trying to behave in other unhealthy ways that you imagine might take the pain away.

Punishing yourself is not the answer. Instead, practice more self-compassion. Tell yourself you are worth more than a thousand rubies. Tell yourself you deserve to be beautiful and happy. Kill all the blame you have targeted towards yourself by forgiving every person who has ever hurt you. Doing all these things might not be easy, but forgiving others and yourself will be easier if you care about yourself.

Never forget this truth —you matter!

BENEFITS OF A LOVING HEART

Do you wonder why I did not say—benefits of a forgiving heart? Here is why. A loving heart encapsulates forgiveness, healing, care, and other good things. Do not just have a compassionate, forgiving heart. Have a heart that loves. More benefits come with your having a loving heart. These benefits can offer more than forgiveness alone:

- You live in peace
- You heal more quickly
- Your blood pressure is lowered
- You have joy even on the worst of days. When your joy is full, you may take the darkest of days and envision the sun's rays shining through. Your joy will be so strong, so powerful, darkness will have no ability to keep you in the night. Your sunrise will come.

- You love yourself

As you have probably heard, "People treat you the way you let them." You attract people with your aura. People are very observant and recognize when someone who hasn't loved them, becomes truly loving, someone who wasn't friendly, becomes friendly. Love and friendliness are like magnets that attract things and people to them. People like to be where they feel loved. Even animals can distinguish this emotion. Do you believe this?

YOUR RELATIONSHIP WITH GOD

The more you delay the moment you forgive whoever hurt you, the more you delay being at peace with God. The lack of a forgiving spirit was a condition I struggled with for most of my teenage years. However, the moment I saw the damage it was doing to my relationship with God, and with my husband, as well, I began to fight it. Getting rid of the grudge became my biggest motivation, determination, and prayer point.

God had helped me see the beauty of living in liberation at that point. He had opened my eyes to what life in Christ meant. I was very anxious to feel the joy of his promises becoming real and evident in my life. So, soon enough, I became purposeful about forgiving. If anyone asked me why I was that intent on fighting away the grudge and pain I carried, I'd tell them it was because I desired to have a more real relationship with God.

This same purpose would be why I'd call my dad and visit him as much as possible. My whole story can be described as the movement of God toward me. God touched my heart and healed me. He took away the pain, anger, and bitterness. He helped me live the very life he wanted me to live.

The beautiful verse in Joel 2:25 is reflected in my life. "I will repay you for the years the locusts have eaten..." Here, God promises to restore all the years that the locusts hath eaten. Indeed, looking back, I can only come to the terms that the enemy stole a lot from me. He placed the blindfold of anger and malice across my eyes and then stole from my potential, time, joy, and much more. However, I am only grateful to God that I was able to give in to forgiveness.

Here is a secret I have not let you in on yet. My father also succumbed to forgiveness. Of course, his change was not spontaneous, but I wasn't willing to relent in my prayers for him. At first, I did not concede by intentionally listening to him and giving him a chance. I did not want to appear to be the weak one. But I learned that yielding to the right things does not mean you are weak. The opposite is true, it means you are strong. And I desperately wanted my dad back.

With mutual forgiveness, we have spent the years since then doing nothing but celebrating the renewal of our relationship. I embrace more than that, my father is now present in my present. He will also be present in my future, and soon enough, we will be able to make memories that cancel out the past.

The future holds more...believe that.

Now, if you have decided on the resolution with which you can build forgiveness, embrace this tip. First, write your purpose in a journal. Journaling is an excellent way of remembrance. Or tell someone about your new resolution, so that he or she can help you be accountable. Second, deciding the month, day, and time when you hope to achieve your purpose may help you remain conscious of your goals and desire to forgive.

REVENGE

I felt driven to talk about revenge because most people who find it hard to forgive have chosen to retaliate against the person who has harmed them in thought, words, or action. The urge to get revenge may get even stronger if people see the same person who hurt them, happy and moving on with his or her life. It is possible for injured persons to look back and get angered because they have not made the progress their offender has.

I understand. I can only imagine how angered I would have been if I heard that my father had remarried and had other kids, that he somehow had caught hold of his life and decided to start again. I would be pushed to retaliate if I caught a glimpse of him laughing with some other daughter or doing the things with her that he had not done with my siblings or me. Revenge would have been my first thought.

However, something about the pain and struggles I have been through would now undoubtedly push me into having second thoughts. Most people never pause to give themselves this chance for reflection. After having those first thoughts of revenge, they immediately take off with their plans.

Have you ever wondered how loyal you might be to your pain and suffering? Really, on thinking twice, I would cancel out my desire for revenge at once. I would not want to hate myself for doing something out of character. I would not want to spend the rest of my life feeding my guilt or living a life of misery.

The Bible directs us not to repay anyone evil for evil. It is God's duty to avenge any wrong situation in which we may find ourselves entangled. God's way is the best. Now, I am not saying we should hope that God will bring evil to those that hurt us. I am saying we should erase the thoughts of anger by taking an unconventional path.

Hope the best for those who have hurt us. This is strange, yes? Through the new understanding that God has given me, if my father found another family to start life over with again, I would only wish his new family the best. I wouldn't want any children to have an absent father, let alone a father who would run away from them when he saw them.

If my father had somehow realized his mistakes, and had come back to us to apologize and promise something better, it would be proof that his life was now guided by the Spirit of God. The Holy Spirit would never let someone who has hurt another person go on with life as if the past had not occurred. Instead, he would urge the person to chase after reconciliation. It would be the person's choice to do so.

If a man like my father had not learned the required lessons, he would face the same issues he had met while sharing his life with us and then would have run away again. If bad habits are not uprooted and released, at some point, they will resurface. Eventually, he would do the same thing he did to us to his new family—run away. Consider how much guilt that would have made him feel. I would not have had to do a single thing to get revenge.

Allow God to defend your cause. Go for anything that will keep the dirty marks out of your slate. Choose things that will protect your heart from the harmful effects of guilt and anger. Choose actions that will put you in the right state with God. Revenge does not make anything better. It may appear to make it better at first, but that is just a band-aid. Never fall for its trick!

CHAPTER 8
The Forgiveness Influence

It is time for us to dig deep. More deeply than we have so far. This reflection requires us to explore our weaknesses, thereby becoming strong. This is the way the empowerment that allows us to surrender still allow us to stand in victory. Ready, set? Here we go!

What techniques can you employ to ensure that you can reach forgiveness? What unseen wounds do you continue to embrace? Is your past your past? Or is your history still running your present life? I wonder if you are unknowingly reacting to deep wounds as I was before I reached out toward forgiveness? What do you think? Here are some essential principles to help you release the negative weights you carry.

LISTENING

Listening well is one skill that can make or break relationships. Strong listening skills are rare because everyone is more interested in being heard. Yet, people are naturally drawn to those who listen well to their cares and stories.

They begin to confide in those who listen, even telling things that shock the listener's soul. The Cambridge Dictionary defines people who will not listen to another person's words as "**ignorant**" and, I would add, selfish. Such people do not seem interested in anyone else but themselves.

Listening is just as significant as speaking. Be sure that you do not make people feel that what they have to say does not matter. Never let others feel any sense of loneliness or isolation. If you do not listen, you may never be able to figure out what went wrong in a relationship. If you ignore essential details, you will ultimately fail to grasp what is truly taking place, and consequently use your imagination to fill in the gaps.

Listening requires commitment and attention. Set aside your values, beliefs, anxieties, and other personal interests in order to listen. When you listen to what someone is saying, your body language should say—I care about your feelings, experiences, and life. Such attentiveness lets you know what people think in their heads, how they feel in their hearts, and how they view the world.

The following DO NOT constitute listening:

- Speaking while others talk
- Faking an interest in what they are saying
- Paying attention to only one detail and ignoring every other one
- Trying to pick out the weak points in a conversation to be able to attack the opposing party
- Checking out your listener's facial expressions to know if you are making an impression

Here are some ideas for improving your listening skills.

- Face the person you are talking to
- Practice active listening (eye contact, paraphrasing what is said and repeating it, verbal affirmations)
- Create a mental picture of the information given
- Refrain from being judgmental
- JUST LISTEN!

Let's practice. Choose someone that you know you can relate to well. When the person is speaking, try your best to ensure you listen to everything they say. Meanwhile, consider a few hindrances to attaining fundamental listening habits:

- **Comparing**: You find listening hard when you begin to make comparisons. When someone speaks to you about themselves, you wonder if you could have dealt with the issue better. Or you say, "If it were me, I would...." Or you conclude with thoughts like these—I have gone through many hardships; he does not know what real hardship is.
- **Mind reading**: A person who tries to read another's mind pays minimal attention to the words uttered and focuses more on the intent he or she imagines behind those words.
- **Rehearsing**: Failing to allow yourself to flow into a conversation will only leave you rehearsing your words: thinking of the next word to utter while faking a look that says you are interested.
- **Filtering**: When you filter out the things someone tells you, you listen to some points while skipping the rest of the details. You find your mind wandering to many other topics.

For example, a mother may listen to her son just long enough to determine if he was hurt. Once she can clarify that, her mind is off to something else.

- **Judging**: This term defines a situation where you judge someone before they get to explain. For example, someone tells you they did drugs when they were a teenager. You stop listening and instantly tag him or her as a horrible person. One of the ways of truly listening is by making your response only after the person speaking has poured out all they want to say.
- **Fantasizing**: Often, we sit right in front of people, and our mind suddenly floats off from the topic to other personal interests. In other words, you "space out." Your mind gets filled with thoughts about a date, work, next project, etc... You must ensure that you find a way to immerse yourself in what you are hearing.
- **Advising**: Most people fall into this bad habit. The other person only tells a little of their story, and already, the listener is thinking of different words of advice. Most people do not want someone who would act as a counselor. They genuinely wish for

someone to stay quiet and listen to everything they need to say.

MEDIATION

Remember, the key to resolving conflict is finding a middle ground; mediation can help you achieve this. Mediation involves a neutral third party to assist in resolving conflict. You may not think you need a mediator, but remember what got you deep in the dispute in the first place. A mediator can help ensure that each of you have an equal opportunity to express yourself.

An experienced, professionally trained mediator knows how to keep things on track so that both sides feel heard and respected. Pastors, therapists, social workers, attorneys, or someone you know that will be fair to both of you can also mediate. It is best to conduct the mediation privately, allowing both sides the safety of being heard without public embarrassment.

Mediation is not appropriate for every situation. Sometimes, hard feelings need more time to heal before mediation is helpful for either party. So, it is important not to rush the process if it does not feel right for you or the other person involved. For example, disputes in which someone has harmed you physically or sexually may be better served by focusing on self-forgiveness through counseling or another form of healing practice before you face the person you need to forgive.

WHY SHOULD WE CARE?

Many of us may spend much of our lives coming to terms with the implications of our past. People find themselves in conflict everywhere: in their homes, at work, and on the internet. One may consider it hard to live in peace and even harder to be at peace with one another. But then, there is the "elephant in the room" that people are too timid to address.

We must accept that discord involves hurting other people. Conflict is a problem because it leads to negative feelings such as anger, fear, sadness, guilt, and shame. It causes stress and wastes time and energy that could be used for more productive activities.

Most conflicts arise out of misunderstandings.

- Misunderstanding of facts.
- Misunderstanding of intentions.
- Misunderstanding of consequences.

WHY DO THESE DISAGREEMENTS HAPPEN?

- People are different from each other.

- People have different opinions, priorities, and needs.
- People are raised in different ways. (i.e., cultural, regional, etc.)
- People communicate differently. The word "No" can be interpreted very differently from person to person.
- People feel threatened by differences.

In Philippians Chapter 4, Apostle Paul writes a letter to the church at Philippi addressing the importance of maintaining unity and peace. Although in a Roman prison at the time, Paul stood as a mediator in the quarrel between Euodia and Syntyche in **Philippians 4:2.**

He wrote in his letter, "I plead with Euodia, and I plead with Syntyche to be of the same mind in the Lord." Paul had previously worked with these women, spreading the gospel throughout the city of Phillipi. It is apparent the disagreement was so strong that Paul heard about it from the prison walls.

Why should we care about this 2000-year-old story? We should care because there is so much more at stake. So much more than egos or feelings. Paul did not take sides. He knew there was something more significant than the argument. He encouraged Euodia and Syntyche to reach a common ground of love, compassion, and peace. There is a greater work to do! So, we cannot be entangled with the "me" syndrome.

> ...make my joy complete by being like-minded, having the same love, being one in spirit and of one mind. Do nothing out of selfish ambition or vain conceit. Rather, in humility, value others above yourselves, not looking to your own interests but each of you to the interests of others.
> **Philippians 2:2-4 NIV**

It is important to understand that you do not always know how someone else feels when you are in a conflict. You cannot tell if that person is hurting by looking at someone's face or body language alone. Sometimes people hide their feelings from you so they do not lose your friendship or affection.

NEGOTIATION

Negotiation can be a decisive step in resolving past incidents so that those involved may move on. It is a strategy to get both parties to say "yes." There can definitely be a win-win in the relationship. To learn how to use your skills to finesse a better relationship, keep reading.

- **Own the problem**

You can be a better negotiator by rethinking your approach to conflict. You must own the problem. What part did you play, if any? Before you ask for what you want, recognize that there may be other ways of looking at the issue. Other people have just as much right to a different opinion. You are looking for solutions, take responsibility, and do not blame or attack.

Understand that if someone feels attacked, one is likely to become defensive. The more defensive one becomes, the less likely it is that one will listen or be willing to resolve the conflict. In such matters, resistance may shut down dialogue altogether. And if you respond by adopting an "attack is my best defense" attitude or strategy, let us just say you will not be demonstrating sound negotiation skills!

- **Make a plan for talking about the problem**

Pause. Think. Speak. Take some time to plan how you want the conversation to go. Ask yourself these questions:

- Am I calm enough to have this discussion?
- Is the other person available and in a good headspace?
- Where is the best place to have this conversation without interruption?
- What do I want out of this conversation?
- What do I think the other person wants out of this conversation?
- How am I going to open the discussion? What are my first sentences going to be?
- Have I thought about what I will say if the other person gets defensive or upset?"

Stay calm and be patient. Although your emotions might feel like they are boiling over, resist the urge to react immediately. Instead of interrupting or responding defensively, exercise patience and give both you and the other person time to voice your concerns. When you hear something upsetting, acknowledge its impact, but do not interrupt until your counterpart concludes speaking.

Stay on topic. It is normal to want to protect yourself by bringing up adverse events from the past. This habit only causes more hurt feelings and resentment in relationships. Instead, begin the conversation on a positive note. This can help ease the tension in the atmosphere.

Do not assume things about each other's feelings or intentions. Assumptions often leave important information obscured. Seeking clarification when necessary helps to validate your understanding. Guessing and getting it wrong only enhances the struggle.

- **What do you want?**

Natalie entered my Christian counseling office. She sat down and immediately began to speak of her troubles. I watched as she moved from side to side, apparently trying but unable to get comfortable. Her fingers were moving around. Her voice continued at a steady pace.

I could see the frustration on her face as her breaths became more rapid. Finally, I stopped her in the middle of a sentence and asked, "Natalie, what do you want?" With a puzzled look, and after a moment of silence, she responded," Well, (pause) I don't know."

No doubt you may have felt this way about some encounter that left your emotions unearthed. You want reconciliation but do not know the specifics of your desires. You are reluctant to speak, supposing that your words may seem irresolute.

Remember, this chapter calls for us to dig deep so the healing process can begin. Be honest with both yourself and the person who has hurt you when you engage in conversation. Ask yourself:

- What do I want to get out of this meeting?
- Do I have a plan for how to react when I don't get what I want?
- What are my priorities for the person on the other side of the table?

These questions all point to one crucial question: what are your hopes for the conversation? Reconciliation if possible. Right? And, perhaps even more important, the ability of both parties to release trapped words and expressions. Even if you do not get everything you want in the resolution, the pressure of unspoken resentments will have been released.

Take some time to create a strategy and to rehearse answers in your mind. And remember, be ready to go with a change in plans if the conversations do not go in the direction you anticipate.

- **Follow up on the discussion**

If the conflict is pending resolution or the person you are working with thinks that a better solution can be reached with further discussion, continue to meet, and find a mutually beneficial solution. To ensure your beginning work does not go to waste, set a date on which you can follow up.

On the next occasion, answer questions like: "Has our situation improved?" "Have there been any other conflicts we have neglected to discuss?" and "What is going well?" If the conflict has not been resolved or has worsened, consider reaching out to an authority figure or other mediator to work through the problem with you.

"If it is possible, as far as it depends on you, live at peace with everyone." Rom 12:18 NIV

Conflict is common but you can reach a mutually satisfying agreement if you handle it well and keep trying. You may even have to agree to disagree. Whether negotiating a raise or planning a trip with your family, it is common to have conflicting thoughts, feelings, and ideas.

Working through forgiveness is no different. It can be uncomfortable, but it is also an opportunity to be heard and to possibly get what you want. If you cannot come up with a solution, try to develop a way for everyone involved to live together peacefully.

Conflict is a regular and healthy part of life. If you never encountered conflict, how would you know how strong, patient, or humble you can be? How would you know the genuineness of peace if there were never any conflicts? And somewhere intertwined in this is forgiveness. To forgive is to choose change and grace despite the conflicts you encounter.

CHAPTER 9
The Fishing Analogy

Growing up, I loved to tag along with my mother when she went fishing—anywhere, anytime, good day or bad. She would get up extra early in the morning as that is when the fish are closer to the warm surface water. She did not believe in catch and release because our dinner depended on the catch.

Early one Saturday morning, I heard a ruffle of sounds. Scrambling to put on my clothes, I rushed outside. She was packing up for a fishing trip and I could not wait to go. We picked up my grandmother along the way and off we went.

Sitting at the shore of the lake, we could see the sun rising from the clouds. The rays gleamed over the water, and a fresh smell was in the air. Suddenly a large fish took my mother's hook and dove down countless yards submerging her fishing cork. I stood and watched as she played the fish cautiously. I sensed my mother analyzing by the look on her face. I thought the line was going to break, but I saw her patiently dig into the long, slow fight.

The cork came up and rested on top of the water. No movement except the ripples in the water. My mother moved the rod and reel from side to side, anticipating the fish was still there. The cork went down into the water again. My mother snapped back on the rod and reel. The fish was firm, trying not to get caught.

"He's a fighter isn't he," my grandmother said. What would mom do? I kept watching. She could keep waiting it out for who knows how long and eventually catch it. Or she could cut the line, releasing herself and the fish, and move on.

Mom's fishing experience reminds my adult self of the situation I experienced with my father. We, adults, come and go as we please. We live where we want and do what we want, right? However, some of us may still be hooked by feelings of pain, heartache, resentment, guilt, or hate from the impact others have had on our lives. We may try to run or suppress these feelings. But no matter where we go or what we do, these unremitting emotional ties persist.

WAITING IT OUT...WHO KNOWS HOW LONG

People find it hard to forgive others even when they want to because of residual emotional pain. Often, the pain could be from someone they trusted the most—a close friend, spouse, parent, etc. A person may remain stuck for a long time wondering how someone they loved and trusted so much was able to hurt them.

Each of us have the same choices in such situations as my mother did with the big fish. One, we can keep waiting for an apology, waiting it out for who knows how long, continuing to hold the pain like cancer slowly spreading. The wound remains raw, open, oozing, and never heals. Our past will dictate future relationships, actions, and our ability to love. Or, two, we can cut the line, releasing ourself and the person who has offended us.

We can choose to accept what happened, then take the necessary steps to break the hold the past has on us. By forgiving my father, I chose the latter and embraced freedom. I was no more the victim but the victor! Before you discover yourself in the scenario described above, consider these pointers:

ANALYZE THE OFFENDER.

Luke 23:34 KJV gives a perfect foundation for this action. "Father, forgive them; for they know not what they do."

What do you think could have made someone who loved you so much become the one to cause you such pain? From my studies, I discovered that most people who wound and betray others do not know what they do. An emotion or a pain may blind the people who hurt you. Sometimes, their blindness exists temporarily. At other times the blinding effects of pain last for years, even decades.

Even though Jesus was hurt and beaten by those he loved, he could still analyze those who wronged him. He went further by asking God to forgive them, an act of true love. He understood that most of his offenders were unaware of their actions' consequences. Viewing the person or situation which causes you suffering, through the lens of "They know not what they do," puts an end to this cycle. It grants your heart permission to still hurt but, more importantly, to forgive.

Once you can understand this, you may be able to defend the cause in support of peace. There are circumstances where you may not be able to understand your offender, let alone want to. It is okay. Just be honest about it. Then, you will find it easier to say these words

— "He did it because he did not understand what he was doing. He did it because he was blinded by his hurt (Remember: Hurt people, hurt people?) and made the mistake of channeling all his frustrations toward me."

Using these words is a sign of empathy and selflessness. You forget about your pain and think of the other's pain.

When I looked into my father's eyes, I saw the soul of a man with years of hurt embedded in his heart. I realized he hadn't wanted my mother to leave with us kids. He loved her. He loved his kids. He just did not know how to make their marriage work.

I defended him as strongly as I had defended my country in the military. He was in his late sixties and walking a little slower by now. Nevertheless, my siblings and I ensured he was well cared for. We defended him and ourselves with unconditional love.

If you are faced with the need to forgive someone, this kind of analysis will help you ensure that you can. Once you understand her or him, you will find it unimportant to hold a grudge. Instead, you will see the other person as someone who needs help, love, and care.

Like my father, other people will be confounded by the love you show. So, you will end up stamping good marks on their hearts. This unconditional act of forgiveness is what we should chase to achieve.

ANALYZE YOUR PAST SINS

When we study all the 'not-so-good' things we did in the past, we find it hard to blame anyone for what they might have done to us. This is because we realize that we have all done something similar or even worse. We recognize that we might have also reacted the same way as the offending party if we had faced the same issue under the same circumstances.

You find forgiving easier when you consider your sins and past experiences. Consider the case of the woman brought before Jesus. She was caught in committing adultery, and her accusers demanded that she be stoned to death according to the laws of Moses. How did Jesus handle this?

He adjured her accusers to analyze their past sins. He summoned the first person without sin to throw a stone at the woman. What do you think happened? No one bent to pick up a rock or talked of throwing one at the woman. They all realized over and over again that they all had committed sins of the same magnitude.

Someone who has tasted God's salvation shouldn't be too hasty to judge those who haven't. If you jog your memory, what do you recall you did in your past? What did you do before you knew Christ? Realize that if you were pure, perfect, and without sin at that time, you would not need to be rescued, restored, or liberated.

ANALYZE THE OUTCOME

The story of Joseph represents an envious beginning but a refined outcome. Genesis 37 recalls how Joseph's brothers sold him as an enslaved person and deceived his father by reporting that vicious animals had killed him. How angry would you feel if you had the same experience? Would you seek a chance at revenge?

Before you answer these questions, peek a little further into Joseph's story. Somehow, God orchestrated Joseph's situation so the brothers would eventually return to ask for his help. They required food as there was a very severe famine in their land.

Joseph's reaction was questionable to his brothers but not to Joseph. He desperately wanted his family back. He desperately wanted his father. Yes, his brothers' behavior stirred up the hurt and pain, but we will learn as we go further.

Joseph had the power to kill them but he chose not to do so. He revealed to them his identity, and instantly, they sank to their knees and began to plead for mercy. Why do you think Joseph didn't get angry?

He was able to analyze the outcome.

"And now, do not be distressed and do not be angry with yourselves for selling me here because it was to save lives that God sent me ahead of you." Gen 45:5 NIV

His words help us realize that he saw a reason for everything that happened. He realized that if his brothers hadn't done what they did to him, he would never have been able to reach the position he was in at that moment. The brothers' acts refined him, and unknown to them and Joseph, they helped him achieve his purpose in life.

Ironically, those who mistreat you may actually help you to climb higher. You may be in the same shoes as Joseph today. You may look back on your life and realize that the incident and pain of the past have refined you and have made you into someone way better. Use that as leverage to achieve forgiveness. Without the suffering you experienced, you might never have become who you are today.

CUT THE LINE

This stage is where we put every detail into practice. Yes, you can call this an impractical moment! It's the actual act of forgiveness where we invest in apology. Yes, invest. When we get to the point where we and the one who hurt us come together, what should we do? What should we possibly expect?

Ask yourself the following questions:

- Was our falling out a result of conflicting ideas?
- Was the person who hurt me facing something that made him unable to realize the wrong he was doing then?
- Were there misconstrued words, expressions, or emotions?

Once you can answer these questions, the forgiveness investment might be easier to achieve.

Now, let us look at the different factors that could cause conflict during a resolution.

- A lack of proper understanding of each other's opinions.

Reason: In most cases, the people who hurt us continue to live as if the painful incident had not occurred. We might make the wrong conclusions regarding the words they say or the expressions they wear.

- One party badgering the other. 'Badgering' describes a scenario where one party intentionally mocks the other.

Reason: Most people do not realize that others do not enjoy being teased. Some try to use teasing to avoid acknowledging their true feelings.

- A disagreement over a fact. Have you ever gotten into a situation where you get angry because someone does not listen to your side of the story?

Reason: Some people caught up in a discussion believe theirs is the only truth, and end up not listening to the other. People often fixate on arguing over facts to avoid tackling deeper issues.

- Disagreements over core values.

Reason: Most people have different values and principles by which they live. Usually, conflicts that arise from this reason may be quite hard to resolve. It is always tough to change a person's integral way of thinking

- Conflicts that arise from ego.

Reason: Most of us admit that we never want to be wrong. We find it hard to accept a loss or defeat in any area of our lives. So, when someone proves to us repeatedly that we are not perfect, we end up resenting their attempts at resolving the conflict.

My mother grappled with the fish for a long time. Finally, she took a small knife out of the tackle box and cut the line releasing herself and the fish from the struggle. Take heart and let go! Cut the line. Your life is too precious to allow hostility to stunt your progress. Make preparations to forgive.

You have been in this chapter of your life long enough. It has caused you much pain; now it is time to turn the page on your past. Turn the page and create better memories. In the final chapter, we will discuss what progress looks like in the journey called Forgiveness.

CHAPTER 10
The Power of Forgiveness

Beth and Jason had been married for fifteen years. Jason had been a truck driver for the last ten years and had spent long days away from home. They had three children, one in junior high and two in elementary school.

Beth also worked as an office administrator for a prominent local company. The physical abuse started after their second child was born. Jason would come home from a three-week absence, red-eyed, ungroomed, exhausted, and stressed—a sure cocktail for a dispute.

On his latest trip, Jason had traveled from Albuquerque, New Mexico, to Memphis, Tennessee. The couple's initial hug was heartfelt. Beth and the kids welcomed daddy home. Jason presented them with gifts from a shop he had visited on his trip.

The family sat at the dinner table as Jason filled them in with stories from his travels. Then he announced that he would be furloughed for the next three months due to the company's vendor contract change. All appeared peaceful for the family reunion, but the familiar noise of discord echoed no sooner than the kids were in bed asleep.

Jason, in an uproar, blamed Beth for not taking the car to get the oil changed. Beth tried to explain how balancing work, kids, and homework had been more challenging the past several weeks. Jason responded with derogatory comments, a shove, and a slap to Beth's face.

Unfortunately, Beth was all too familiar with nights like this. Even when her husband was away, she witnessed her son emulating his father's actions toward her daughters. Beth was desperate for a release.

Jason slept in the following day. The kids were off to school, and Beth delayed reporting to work for about two hours. She wanted to do something nice for Jason, so she prepared breakfast and began doing his laundry.

Sifting through his pant pockets, she noticed the white substance—cocaine. Jason's struggle with cocaine off and on had almost led Beth to file for divorce. Repeatedly she forgave him, admitting she chose to stay because of her children.

She confided in two of her best friends, Carol and Jessica, who agreed that she should divorce Jason but also wanted to support their sister in need. They began sharing Beth's workload amongst themselves. They prayed with her and often cooked a meal to lift her burdens. Two more months went by with no change from Jason. Beth was grateful to her friends, but, one day, exhausted from the grace she bestowed on her husband, she walked into a lawyer's office.

As the process began, Beth was nervous, and fearful. But she felt easier as she crossed the "t" to finalize her signature on the document. Her lawyer counseled her on how to deliver the message to her husband. Beth absorbed his words.

She contacted her friends to tell them of her decision. She would tell Jason before the kids arrived home from school. Carol offered to pick the children up and take them to her house. Jessica said she would be nearby if any need arose. Beth's plan was in motion.

She entered her home to find Jason standing at the dining room table with the packaged cocaine lying on the table. His face was swollen, and his eyes were drenched with tears. "I'm sorry," he said, "I'm sorry. What I've done isn't right, and I'm sorry. You've forgiven me too many times for me to keep living like this." They both sat at the dining room table, and after a long talk,

Jason opted for counseling for himself first, then for him and Beth, then for the whole family.

Together they disposed of the substance, and Jason promised never to touch it again. Beth believed Jason's words were truly from his heart, so she delayed the divorce and chose reconciliation. With apprehension, Carol and Jessica supported Beth's decision; however, they continued to stand with her in the fight for her family.

Grace is free, but trust is earned. Some people have difficulty forgiving one another because they do not trust that the other will change. They assume that someone's past behavior is the primary indicator of what they will do in the future. Others think forgiving early on is too soon as the wound is still freshly open. Trust yourself to create a boundary without giving people unlimited access to your heart.

SELF-FORGIVENESS

Just as forgiving others means letting go of the emotions associated with the harm the other has done to you, forgiving yourself means letting go of the emotions associated with the realization that you, too, were at fault. Each person must acknowledge having made a mistake for self-forgiveness, reconciliation, and restitution to occur.

Take note, acknowledging your mistake does not take away from your worth or from your values. As long as I thought my dad was the only one responsible for our situation, he and I could never achieve a forgiving relationship. Looking at the big picture, I conjured up negative judgments in my mind that caused my heart to harden.

Forgiveness comes easily to some people, but others must work at it. It is important to remember that forgiveness is a process, not a one-time event. It is a vertical decision lived out horizontally. Your brain must rewire to forgiveness.

Throughout this book, I have given you nuggets to ponder as you prepare to forgive. Below is a roundup of the thoughts and strategies that will help you bring someone to the point where they can make amends and you can forgive them and yourself and you both can realize that you are human and deserve forgiveness.

- Put yourself in the other person's shoes. See their situation through their eyes and try to understand how they feel. For instance, you may feel hatred as the victim of a robbery. However, you may become merciful if you learn that the thief could not pay their rent and their children needed food.

- Think about why the other person acts or reacts the way they do. Remember the book's title, *"Hurt People, Hurt People"*? Now think about why you act or react the way you do. Can you prevent negative actions in the future?
- If you are unwilling to forgive yourself, you must find out why. Be willing to ask yourself tough questions and be ready to answer truthfully. You may be able to forgive, eventually, but not be able to bear that cross right now.
- The more insight you gain, the better your chances of understanding yourself, your offender, and possibly reconciling with both down the road.

As you begin to heal, it is essential to acknowledge the feelings that you might have, but do not overthink them. People who have experienced hurt in the past may find it harder to forgive those who do similar things to them in the present. For example, people who have been consistently lied to by a loved one may struggle with trusting other people or feeling comfortable developing other close personal relationships.

The following Alphabet of Forgiveness might help you remember the strategies we have discussed:

A—Action. Act now!

B—Believe. Believe in yourself. You can do it!

C—Counsel. Seek counsel if needed.

D—Develop compassion.

E—Expose unforgiveness.

F—Faith and Freedom. Work toward these.

G—Give forgiveness.

H—Health and Hope. Remember, these are your goals.

I—If in doubt, forgive anyway.

J—Joy. Remember, this will be the result of forgiveness.

K—Know that you are forgiven.

L—Love, Live, and Let go!

M—Mindset Change. Can you accomplish this?

N—Now, not tomorrow.

O—Open your heart to forgive.

P—Pray, Persist, and be Patient.

Q—Quit dwelling on the past.

R—Replace grudges with Generosity. Repent, change your ways.

S—Something better awaits you.

T—Trust the process and be Thankful.

U—Understanding the other and yourself will ease your path.

V—Vision. See yourself as forgiving and forgiven.

W—Wisdom is what you will gain, when you walk the journey to forgiveness.

X—(X-ray) Examine yourself.

Y—Yield.

Z—Zeal. If you seek to forgive and be forgiven with zeal, you WILL NOT pass on your pain to others.

A FINAL WORD

Breathe!

Yes, we have come to the end of the winding labyrinth of forgiveness. I will emphasize again that forgiveness is not a one-time thing. It is also not an action you take spontaneously. Every day, you choose to forgive. You choose a fulfilled and happy life for yourself. You choose to free your heart from its chains.

Now, I understand that this journey may be hard. Along the way, you may feel the same anger you felt at the time you were first wounded all over again and with even more agony. This is the point where you will purposely give in to God.

Let forgiveness reign!

Yes, I would still like to change my past, well, at least, part of it. But then I must ask myself if I would be the same person I am today. So whatever went wrong, release it. If you cannot release it, let it empower you to do something better. Start a new chapter in your book about yourself. You are the main character, but let God be the Author and you take the role of Co-Author.

My parents had their own separate pasts, which came together but separated again. My mother did the best she could to raise four children while single. As a result, my siblings and I grew up to be respectful and hardworking, with spirituality and a tightly knitted bond. The Bible commands us to honor our father and mother (Exodus 20:12, Ephesians 6:2). I believe we have done this unto the Lord.

My dad and I became Father and Daughter when I was thirty-seven. God is an interesting Orchestrator of life. "Dad is in the hospital", my sister, Gina said, "He had a stroke."

Now, I could have been revengeful and said, he is reaping what he has sown (Don't think badly of me. You might have said this yourself). But instead, I remembered the words of my mother, "No matter what, he is still your dad." I loved him so much that the only thing I wanted to do was to take care of him.

We four siblings purposefully united. We took care of him with love, prayer, and humility. From the doctor to the barber shop, from the bank to the grocery store, each of us took turns. Dad hosted many holiday gatherings at my grandmother's house, which became his home.

The former years of sadness and anger were replaced with laughter of joy and peace. My eyes fill with tears even as I write this paragraph. Unfortunately, Dad passed away July 2021. Yet, I believe that, before he died, we had loved him to LIFE because our "latter days" with him were better than the former days. We wrote new chapters in our life's book.

Here is a side note. If the one who has hurt you has died before you have reconciled, you can still forgive them. Here is an exercise I implemented during my counseling sessions. Write the offender a letter. In the body of the letter, express your hurt, pain, bitterness, anger, resentment, etc. In the conclusion, it is crucial to write the words, "I FORGIVE YOU" and to list the offenses you are forgiving.

After you finish writing the letter, place two empty chairs in a quiet room. Sit in one chair and imagine the deceased offender in the other. (I have also heard of this taking place by the dead offender's gravesite.) Read the letter while facing the empty chair. If you need to stand and yell, scream or cry, you are free to do so. Make sure you are in front of the offender's chair at the letter's end.

Once the exercise is complete, you may destroy the letter as you see fit. Deep breath. Exhale. The past is in the past. The future has come.

I have learned to let go. The weight of not forgiving was too heavy for me to bear. My parents were not the perfect parents, but neither was I the perfect child. My mother was my hero! She survived the years with four teenagers in the house. LOL! But my dad was my hero too. He also learned to let go.

Although alcohol had power over my dad's life for decades, it DID NOT have the final authority. The stroke opened my dad's eyes and heart to what mattered: his relationship with God, family and life itself. As a result, he became sober and stayed sober until his last breath.

In his book, Forgiving Our Parents, Dwight L. Wolter said, "Letting go is an integral part of forgiveness". He added:

"We can admit to ourselves that, try as we may, the past cannot be undone. We can let go of our hope for a better yesterday."

Remember, forgiveness promotes freedom. It does not always lead to friendship and reconciliation. You can forgive those you need to stay far away from, perhaps including some family members. You may not forget the hurt that happened to you, but the memory may stop it from happening again.

One has to let go and move on with one's life. I got angry with my father for leaving, and for a long time, I struggled to achieve balance in my life. This led me to a rollercoaster of mistrust and unforgiveness toward others.

My pain left my present moments defensive. I could not leave myself vulnerable. When I reached the end of myself, I went for the help of God. With his help, I found my way to forgiveness and reconciliation. Today, I am a better person. The past may not have played out well, but I have a whole future in view. Dad and I had time to build on what we lost. I am glad the Lord had proven himself faithful by causing restoration between us.

My friend, this could be your story. Like me, many people go through life looking for everyone else to be perfect while ignoring the one in the mirror looking back at them. Pain, whether physical, emotional, or spiritual, and sin, intentional or unintentional, are too heavy for us to carry.

Hurt is still hurt, whether from one's parents, siblings, teacher, pastor/church, friend, or boss. Matthew 5:44 tells us to pray for our enemies; at times, any of the people close to us may fit the bill. So how do we forgive someone while our broken heart is still mending? We let go of the lie of perfection and embrace the truth!

The best way I can think of to close this journey we have taken together is to invite you to turn to God as you struggle with your own forgiveness.

The following prayers will guide you into the prayer of forgiveness, releasing you from the burdens that keep you from living a victorious life. You may personalize these prayers by inserting the name of the one that hurt you. Allow the words to sink in, and—in the words of my wise grandmother—"You take one step, God will take two." You can do this, my friend!

Prayers, joy, and peace to you! ~ Cassie

"Get rid of all bitterness, rage and anger, brawling and slander; along with every form of malice. Be kind to one another, tenderhearted, forgiving one another; as in Christ God forgave you." Ephesians 4:31-32 NIV

"He has removed our sins as far from us as the east is from the west." Psalm 103:12 NLT

Prayers

Our Father, which art in heaven,
   Hallowed be thy name.
   Thy kingdom come. Thy will be done in earth, as it is in heaven.
   Give us this day our daily bread.
   And forgive us our debts (sin), as we forgive our debtors (offenders).
   And lead us not into temptation, but deliver us from evil:
   For thine is the kingdom, and the power, and the glory, forever. Amen.
   ~ Matt 6:9-13 Life in the Spirit Bible (emphasis added)

MY PERSONAL PRAYER

Dear Father, thank you for another chance to reflect on where I am and to know that I need you.

Forgive me for not thanking you enough for who you are and what you have done in my life. Lord, forgive me of my sins. I don't deserve your forgiveness, but because of your unconditional love, your Word says that you will forgive me.

Thank you for giving me love instead of resentment, mercy instead of justice, your presence instead of abandonment. Father it is not always easy to forgive or forget the hurt others have done to me. Holding on to this pain has caused me to suffer and miss your blessings in my life. I surrender my unforgiveness to you, Father.

Help me to forgive and let go of bitterness, anger, malice, hate, etc., that filled my heart because I chose not to forgive. Teach me to lay down my rights and extend forgiveness to others as you have bestowed forgiveness on me. Give me the strength to trust you. Help me to remember how much you love and care for me and how much I have been forgiven.

Grant me the freedom that comes with forgiveness. Bring healing to my heart and the hearts of those I have hurt and those who have hurt me. I am not the judge, so I trust you, God, to deal with the person who wronged me. Please help me to be at peace with your ruling. Thank you, Father. In Jesus's Name. Amen.

FORGIVE YOURSELF

"Father, today I ask forgiveness of all the negative and harmful words I have spoken about myself. I do not want to abuse myself in such a way again. Transform my thoughts and let me understand how marvelously you made me. Change my habits, so I use my tongue to speak hope and favor upon my life. In Jesus' name." ~ Sarah Coleman, Woman's Day Magazine www.womansday.com

STRUGGLE TO FORGIVE

"Merciful God, My heart is struggling to forgive the person who hurt me. It feels like I am letting them off the hook if I forgive them. It's as though justice will never be served. But You have said vengeance is Yours, not mine to take upon myself. Lord, your word tells me to forgive others as you have forgiven me, but I just can't seem to forgive them fully. I am struggling to move forward from this pain. Please change my heart, Lord. Help me to trust your way and to live free from bitterness." ~ In Jesus' matchless name, Amen. (adapted from Charismatic Episcopal Church)

"Dear Merciful Lord,

Thank you for your gift of forgiveness. Your only Son loved me enough to come to earth and experience the worst pain imaginable so I could be forgiven. Your mercy flows to me in spite of my faults and failures. Your Word says to "clothe yourselves with love, which binds us all together in perfect harmony." (Col. 3:14) Help me demonstrate unconditional love today, even to those who hurt me.

I understand that even though I feel scarred, my emotions don't have to control my actions. Father, may your sweet words saturate my mind and direct my thoughts. Help me release the hurt and begin to love as Jesus loves..... The rest of this prayer can be found at *https://www.crosswalk.com/faith/prayer/a-prayer-for-forgiving-those-who-hurt-you.html*

Helpful Resources

National Domestic Violence Hotline 1-800-799-7233

National Child Abuse Hotline 1-800-422-4453

National Alcoholism and Substance Abuse Information Center 1-800-784-6776

References

Chapter 2

Kenneth E. Hagin. Exceedingly Growing Faith. Kenneth Hagin Ministries. January 1973

Martin Luther King, Jr. https://www.goodreads.com/quotes/57037-forgiveness-is-not-an-occasional-act-it-is-a-constant attitude.

Chapter 3

Heidi Moawad, MD. https://www.neurologylive.com/view/neurobiology-forgiveness. Article September 24, 2018 (assessed October 18, 2022).

https://healthcare.utah.edu/healthfeed/postings/2017/02/relationships.php Ferbuary 14, 2017. Office of Public Affairs

https://www.coolnsmart.com/quote-the-only-time-you-should-look-down-8913/

Chapter 4

Kenneth E. Hagin. Exceedingly Growing Faith. Kenneth Hagin Ministries. January 1973

Chapter 5

Kenneth E. Hagin. Exceedingly Growing Faith. Kenneth Hagin Ministries. January 1973

Chapter 6

https://www.opentohope.com/forgive-for-good. Article 2008 Accessed July 21, 2022

Crystal Raypole. How to Forgive Someone: Even If They Really Screwed Up. Article https://www.health line.com/health/how-to-forgive#moving-forward Nov 19, 2019

Chapter 7

Eric Jaffe https://www.psychologicalscience.org/observer/the-complicated-psychology-of-revenge October 4, 2011

Crystal Raypole. How to Forgive Someone: Even If They Really Screwed Up. Article https://www.healthline.com/health/how-to-forgive#moving-forward Nov 19, 2019

Chapter 8

Matthew McKay, Patrick Fanning, and Martha Davis. Messages: The Communication Skills Book. New Harbinger Publications, 4th ed. August 1, 2018.

https://corporatefinanceinstitute.com/resources/careers/soft-skills/improve-your-listening-skills/ article 2022 (accessed October 10, 2022)

Stephanie A. Sarkis, PhD. "Do We Really Need to Forgive." https://www.psychologytoday.com/us/blog/here-there-and-everywhere/202103/do-we-really-need-forgive Article (accessed June 12, 2022)

William Park. "What Other Cultures Can Teach Us About Forgiveness. Article www.bbc.com November 9, 2020. (accessed November 19, 2022)

Isaiah Majinbon. "Alternative Dispute Resolution" Article. (Mediation) www.studocu.com/my/document/universiti-malaya/alternative-dispute-resolution/alternative-dispute-resolution/35769303 2018

Chapter 9

Robert Enright. "Eight Keys to Forgiveness". https://greatergood.berkeley.edu/article. October 15, 2015

Frederic Luskin, Ph.D. "Forgive for Good: The Four Stages of Forgiveness", Article https://www.opentohope.com/forgive-for-good/ 2008 (accessed July 21, 2022)

Chapter 10

Dag Heward-Mills. Forgiveness Made Easy. Parchment House Publishers. September 24, 2017

Dwight L. Wolter, Forgiving Our Parents (Minneapolis, MN: CompCare, 1989) pg. 55-56

Other books by the Author

Author Cassie can be reached at:

www.cassiejwilliams.org

cassiewilliams1818@gmail.com

About Cassie Williams

Cassie J. Williams, PhD, is a Navy veteran, Life Coach, Motivational Speaker, and Chaplain. She is passionate about empowering Kingdom growth. She travels nationwide teaching women in prisons, Dream centers, and safe houses their self-worth and identity in Christ.

Cassie's genuine approach and compassion help her connect with people from all walks of life. She is a graduate of Liberty University and resides in Texas with her husband and children.

www.ingramcontent.com/pod-product-compliance
Lightning Source LLC
Chambersburg PA
CBHW032117090426
42743CB00007B/380